DOUBLE EXPOSURE

DOUBLE EXPOSURE

DOUBLE
DOUBLE

WILLIAM MORROW & CO., INC./NEW YORK

EXPOSURE
EXPOSURE

RODDY McDOWALL

Library of Congress Catalog Card Number: 90-53187

ISBN: 0-688-10062-7

Printed in Japan

Second Edition

2 3 4 5 6 7 8 9 10

CONTENTS
CONTENTS

DOUBLE EXPOSURE
DOUBLE EXPOSURE

I WOULD RATHER see her smoke a cigarette than spend a day in a museum. She smokes it with passion, humor, grace, hunger!

To watch Simone is a joy—the actress supreme, the complete woman involved in the exciting business of living!

SIMONE SIGNORET
BY ROSALIND RUSSELL

REX HARRISON
BY BEATRICE LILLIE

R EX HARRISON has long impressed cinema and theatre
audiences, as well as myself, with his consistently
adept and highly professional approach to his art—
be the vehicle romantic, dramatic or comedic.

I rate him among the very few who command such
versatility. One rarely finds a dramatic actor who
so successfully scales the difficult peaks of high comedy.

To wax poetic:

> HARRISON, REX
>
> HIGGINS
>
> CAESAR
>
> and sex
>
> TO NAME A FEW
>
> THAT WILL DO
>
> TO DEMONSTRATE
>
> HOW WE RATE THIS FINE COMIC THESP
>
> WHOSE TIMING'S A FACTOR
>
> IN TURNING OUR HEADS.

SAMMY DAVIS, JR.
BY ANTHONY NEWLEY

To BE PERFECTLY HONEST with you, Sammy Davis frightens me. I mean, anyone with all that talent must be in league with the devil or something! You see, I have this theory about "star" quality. I think great actors tend to cover themselves up (characterization and stuff), whereas the great star literally strips himself naked. For a few pennies they allow us the privilege of gawking at their insides. A lot of them do it without meaning to. They seem to have no defense mechanism at all. Marilyn Monroe, for example. Other performers, like Sam, who began in show business as children seem to have whittled this "self-exposure" bit down to a fine art. They seem to have *dropped* the façade that most performers "adopt" when they perform.

To be present when Sammy Davis performs on a café floor is to watch the raw, bleeding human animal. There seems to be no artifice at all. (The pinnacle of art?) You can *feel* his heartbeat from your ringside table. I can't think of any other performer today who evokes such a feeling of "relationship" with an audience. That incredible "nakedness" of the superb artist coupled with giant versatility. An unbeatable combination! He sings and dances, knocks off a solo or two on any number of musical instruments, does brilliant, brilliant impressions of other well-known performers, and, for good measure, he'll round off the evening with a display of lightning finger tricks with a pair of six-shooters! Damn it, sir! He's a walking Ed Sullivan Show!

For a start, where does he get all that energy? (To spend an evening on the town with Sam is like hanging onto the tail of a comet.) He has a "side" talent for work that would do justice to a cart horse. He's the easiest touch in the business for a charity concert or a benefit or fund-raising dinner, and all this on top of a heavy professional schedule.

What makes Sammy run so hard? Well, there's a lot of easy psychological game playing to be had over Sam's hidden drives. You know the sort of thing. Negro kid "born in a trunk," "back of the bus" bit. (It's uncanny how much great talent springs from misery!) And then again, "Sammy has to prove himself all the time!". . ."He wants the whole world to love

him!" If this is true, Sam's gonna have to move over and make room for the rest of us in show business.

Becoming a friend of Sam's means joining the rest of his *mishpucha* and shaking your head a lot and clucking like an old Dutch uncle and muttering, "Why does he have to work so hard? Why doesn't he take it easy?"

I was in his dressing room one day when Sam was discussing union business with some friends from the American Guild of Variety Artists. Suddenly Sam turned to me and said, "I'm running for President!" He meant President of AGVA, of course, but I thought he meant of the United States! And I remember thinking, Yes—and he'll *get in* too, if he wants!

No, there is *no* one—repeat, *no* one—in the world like him today. And that's *world*, Charlie Brown!

"Ladies and gentlemen, it gives me great pride and pleasure to present that lovable, exasperating, cuddly, infuriating, childlike, raw, richly encrusted whirlwind performer—the one and only. . . Sammy Davis!" (Music and hysterical applause.)

I tell you he frightens me. Anyone with that much going for him must be in cahoots with the devil!

MARGARET LEIGHTON
BY TERENCE RATTIGAN

To KNOW Margaret Leighton is not necessarily to love her; to know her well is to adore her. To meet she can be a little forbidding. How often have I sat in her dressing room and held my breath as some unwary but worshiping visitor has told her how "marvelous, but simply marvelous" he has found her performance. If there has been even the faintest hint of going too far or of flattery in the words—and, let's face it, in most dressing-room congratulations there usually is— then the poor man will get one of two answers, both delivered in the flattest of carefully recalled Midlands accent. Either it will be:

"Don't talk (nonsense). I was (simply) awful tonight."

(I have parenthesized two words which don't figure largely in Margaret's vocabulary. Your readers may search for more colorful alternatives and no doubt they will find them.)

Or else it will be, perhaps even more disconcertingly:

"Yes, I suppose I wasn't too lousy tonight" and then a happy smile of reminiscence will disperse the gloom of so shameful an admission. "Ah! But last night I was simply terrible! simply excruciating! Ask Terry. He'll tell you."

And I usually will, preferring peace to truth.

Margaret, you see, is a perfectionist, superbly professional, ruthlessly self-critical. For her the backstage chi-chi of pretty flowers and pretty compliments is anathema. She wants only the truth, and honestly prefers the uncomfortable truth to the comfortable, for comfort leads to complacency and complacency to a bad performance, and a bad performance, despite her fervent and profane assurances to the contrary, is something that Margaret will never and can never give.

In private life she is a bundle of amiable contradictions. Rather shy, but perfectly capable of putting something on her head that will quench all conversation at the Colony for an hour. Rather neglectful of her friends, until they need her help—when she has, quite often, to be forcibly restrained from dying for them. Never appearing to read a book or newspaper, but always seeming to know much more about Rhodesia or Proust than you do. A slim sapling seemingly bent agonizingly double by the mildest emotional breeze; but when a hurricane strikes, a stout, unwavering oak.

Happily she looks far more like a slim sapling than a stout, unwavering oak, which is perhaps the slightest of the reasons why I, and indeed all who really know Margaret, adore her.

JACK BENNY
BY CHARLES SCHULZ

LAUREN BACALL
BY KATHARINE HEPBURN

SOFT AND SLEEK—and looking—looking . . . Sloe-eyed—moving through the words on a carpet of wet brown leaves (or anyway a carpet—the best—and long—and deep) . . . No sound—only a rhythmic beat . . . Honey dripping from her temples . . . Eyes unblinking—glinting green—challenging . . . Her texture bread-dough soft—and smooth and tawny—rising alive . . . He has penned in a lioness . . . No claws for those she loves—babies—mate—and even friends—a few . . . The best—the best (what the hell—they must be—they're mine) . . . You are subdued by her lavish enthusiasm—lulled by the repetition of your own extraordinary virtues . . . You are a king among mice—secure—remarkable—you have no equal . . . You belong to the kingdom of her children— she will protect you . . . But if you do not belong: look out . . . No zulac from the bazaar has a sharper knife—can use it without pause—direct—piercing . . . Love or Hate . . . Yes or No . . . Good or Bad . . . Victorian clarity . . . Soft—sun-serene surface—surface—surface—and under it—Woman.

BROOKS ATKINSON
BY AL HIRSCHFELD

SOME YEARS AGO I received a phone call from the proprietor of the Mansfield Theatre, located on West 47th Street in New York City. The ensuing dialogue ran something like this:

MIKE: Hello, Al? This is Mike Myerberg. I'm calling to ask your advice on a very sticky problem. D'you have a minute or shall I call—

ME: No. No, go ahead . . . . I'm free.

MIKE: Well . . . it's like this. I'm seriously thinking of changing the name of my theatre from the Mansfield to the Brooks Atkinson Theatre. I believe this would be the first time a theatre was named after a drama critic—but that's not the main point. Y'see, Al, I've always had a profound respect for Brooks and I'd like to publicly honor him for his great contribution to the creative talents and culture of this country.

ME: Sounds great. What's the problem?

MIKE: Well . . . you're an old friend of his, and I want you to level with me. How do you think Brooks would react to this? Do you think he would be embarrassed?

ME: Embarrassed? Good God, no! I've never heard anything so insane . . . and besides, he's retired as drama critic, so it's not as though you were using his name for special—

MIKE: Yes, yes, I know. I just don't want to offend him, that's all. Y'know how Brooks is. Think about it, Al, and call me back, or better still—sound him out when you see him. No, no, that's no good. It may seem as though we were gossiping about him behind his back. What d'you think about my calling him direct and saying, straight out, "Brooks, would you mind if I renamed my theatre after you?"

The above conversation may seem pure fantasy, but it is the unvarnished truth. In the normal course of events, the question of whether or not anyone would be embarrassed by having a city, monument or theatre named after him seems remote—unless the recipient of the accolade happened to be Brooks Atkinson; then it would be perfectly normal to consider his feelings in the matter. You just don't name a theatre after Atkinson without first finding out how he feels about it.

In a recent issue of *Times Talk*, a house organ published by *The New York Times*, John Canaday, art oracle for the *Times*, recorded his impressions of Brooks Atkinson: "It has been five years now that I've been sitting around *The New York Times* twiddling my thumbs and watching how the place operates, and I think somebody should tell the truth about Brooks

26

BROOKS ATKINSON
BY AL HIRSCHFELD

Atkinson. After all, the guy isn't God and it's high time somebody said so." Canaday's searching appraisal continues its speculative fancy by listing some of the imponderables in Atkinson's makeup. First, his name, "Brooks," with its double meaning—haberdashery and babbling—then his uncanny stamina in attending opening nights for a million years . . . or his use of elementary English language to cunningly create the illusion of erudition . . . perhaps his boyhood experience as sound-effects man in some remote New England nickelodeon accounts for it all. Could it be his intimacy with birds rather than Broadway chicks? Maybe it's his ability to fool everyone around the place, even including his devoted secretary, Clara Rotter, merely by sitting there at his desk under that mop of hair, with that pipe and tweed jacket. Whatever the reasons, implausible and improbable as they may seem, the fact remains, as Mr. Canaday sums up in his profile with the suggestion: "But why not face things and change the name to the *Times-Atkinson*?"

Ah, there, Mr. Canaday, is where you are in obvious error. I have no quarrel with your estimate and shrewd analysis of what makes Mr. Atkinson tick. But your solution is out of the question. For having publicly announced changing the New York *Times* to the *Times-Atkinson* has forever doomed this otherwise sane, reasonable and long-overdue honor from any further consideration. You neglected to ask Brooks in advance how he felt about it! Perhaps we could meet one day for lunch and discuss (privately) the possibility of changing Broadway into the Brooks Atkinson Avenue, and then Off Broadway would automatically become the Off-Atkinson Theatre. How's about it?

JULIE HARRIS
BY CHRISTOPHER ISHERWOOD

HOW WOULD I describe Julie Harris? What is the particular quality of her genius as an actress? I think of two words, *delight* and *defiance*. How unforgettably, in *I Am a Camera*, she spoke the line, "Oh, this is wonderful—even *warm*, it's wonderful!" Actually, she was just referring to a bottle of champagne which hadn't been put on ice. Yet she managed to conjure up the innermost magic of pleasure. She thrilled us with her delight. A genius for delight implies its opposite, of course. Julie's white face—it turns death-white, not merely pale, as if utterly drained by her emotional ebbtide—can express the blankness of terminal despair. Not for long, however. For it is unthinkable that she could ever be really defeated. Her sword is whipped from its scabbard, flashing the signal to attack; it points to the enemy position against which she will lead us. . . . I remember how, once, through a misunderstanding, she thought I had said to her, "How dare you?" (As if I could ever have been so foolish!) Immediately, she sprang to her feet, exclaiming, "I dare what I will!"—a magnificently spontaneous cry of defiance which might well be the motto of some ancient family of warriors. Yes, no matter whether she is playing Juliet or Nora, Queen Victoria or Sally Bowles, Julie is always also Joan of Arc.

DICK VAN DYKE
BY CARL REINER

T H E Y : "What's Dick Van Dyke really like?
He seems to be a very decent human being."

M E : He is.

T H E Y : "He seems to be very easy to work with."

M E : He is.

T H E Y : "It seems that his comedy comes effortlessly
and intuitively."

M E : It does.

M E : Dick Van Dyke is the only comedian extant who is
equally brilliant in performing light romantic
comedy and low slapstick comedy. I dare you to
name one in the world who is his equal.

NOËL COWARD
BY BETTY COMDEN
AND ADOLPH GREEN

MAYBE IT WAS because this girl from Brooklyn and this boy from the Bronx were the two young hopefuls most-unlikely-ever-to-be-cast-in-a-Noël-Coward-play that made us constantly visualize ourselves appearing in one—elegantly dressed and tossing off those glass-brittle lines in perfect, clipped accents. Stemming more from the milieu of Studs Lonigan's "world I never made," we felt Noël Coward represented the "world we never *could* make," our distinctly non-British noses pressed against the French windows, eyes peering hungrily at the devastating figures inside. Betty: "I'm Victoria . . . Victoria Marsden. I'm afraid you're terribly attractive." Adolph: "My name is Simon . . . Simon Gayforth. I love you . . . desperately." Those were some of the first lines we ever wrote (?) in a sketch for our satiric night-club act, "The Revuers." We were making fun, but for a moment we were *there*—in a Mayfair drawing room, or on a terrace overlooking the Riviera. And what did we always pick to do for auditions at the American Theatre Wing, in an understandably futile attempt to be noticed? *Red Peppers*, of course. ("Now then." . . . "Now then what?" . . . "Now then, "*what?*'*!!!*") Or the first scene of *Private Lives*, involving the Duke of Westminster's ubiquitous yacht. At that time, school meant studying only Shakespeare, Shaw and Sheridan, and it was good for you also to watch man's valiant struggle in the toils of the Depression, lyricized in Odets' *Awake and Sing* and presented by the stunning acting company of the Group Theatre. But still you sneaked off for evenings of heady excitement standing tirelessly at the back of the theatre, gorging yourself on the nectar and ambrosia of *Tonight at 8:30*. Then there was the movie *The Scoundrel*, not written by him, true, but what a performance! We saw it so many times we learned it by heart, and spent many long bus and subway rides tossing each other cues. And with similarly "Coward-crazy" friends we would have "Scoundrel" parties, at which we all would re-enact the entire film.

Noël's phrases from the movie slipped easily into our daily conversation. Getting up from a cafeteria table, it was customary for one of us to say, "Much as I hate stooping to symbolism . . ." and drown a crumpled napkin in a tumbler of water, giving a totally unrecognizable imitation of Noël dousing a white flower in a highball glass to signify the end of an affair. Or on being told by an acquaintance that he was about to marry the girl of his dreams, one of us might state in the waspish tones of Alexander Woollcott (from the same picture), "An interesting revenge." The other would parry (as Noël), "It will be a perfect match. Two empty paper bags belaboring each other." Small wonder our circle of acquaintances dwindled . . . but never our admiration for Noël and everything in *The Scoundrel*, including a restaurant called the Hapsburg House, where a charming dinner—love scene was shot. In fact, I (Betty) went so far as to have my own wedding luncheon there.

Many years after all this we met Noël Coward at Gene Kelly's house in Beverly Hills. More often than not, an evening at the Kellys' was strictly a sweat-shirt-and-slacks festival, but for this occasion, feeling sure that the guest of honor would be attired in at least dinner jacket and solar topee, everyone got into something a bit more formal. Finally he arrived. He had on a crumpled tweed jacket and a bow tie, but still looked exactly like Noël Coward. His eyes quickly took in the room. He lowered his eyelids and murmured in a characteristically ironic

NOËL COWARD
BY BETTY COMDEN
AND ADOLPH GREEN

monotone, "You're all so elaborately done up. I'm afraid I feel frightfully shabby!" The impact, and what it meant to us, is hard to describe, as was the thrill of hearing him perform his own marvelous material till eight the next morning.

From then on we got to know each other well enough to send, on various occasions, telegrams referring to certain obscure poets he had invented for an hilarious anthology called *Spangled Unicorn*. Wires passed between us signed "Crispin Pither," "A. E. Maunders" and "Albrecht Drausler." One of them came to us at the Cherry Lane Theatre a few years back, when we were opening in our one-man, one-woman show, *A Party*. And along with it came a phone call which the girl in the box office answered. Voice: "Hallo. This is Noël Coward. You're holding a ticket for me for tonight, dear girl? Well, a friend of mine just got in from London and phoned me from the airport. I insisted he come *directly* down to see the show, so *do* be a dear and set aside another ticket, won't you, in the name of Sir Laurence Olivier?" The poor girl fainted dead away. The whole Cherry Lane Theatre shook and sent off rockets. In our tiny dressing room, we, too, felt just as shaken. Knowing that someone you once long admired from afar admires *you* is a lovely feeling.

Noël was a light to us. He opened doors. To us he represented "class"—and we don't mean that in the superficial sense. We mean the highest of wit, of style, of discipline and craftsmanship, plus a truly unique talent and personality both as writer and performer. His candor, his irreverence, his impatience with falseness, his sharpness are well known. Happily we have also seen his warmth, his kindness, and shared some small portion of his friendship. It is comforting to know that after all these years his mother country is finally beginning to recognize the enduring value and brilliance of his theatre works. We knew it all the time.

ED WYNN
BY RED SKELTON

HIS PERSONAL encouragement, when I was but a small boy, made him my friend. His goodness and kindness made me love him.

Ed Wynn had a greatness beyond words. He had a humanity about him that you felt. He was like a giant oak with happy children playing beneath him. All the goodness that can come from the simple things in life, that bring joy and laughter, had been placed in the heart of Ed Wynn.

With the clown, the wondering spirit of comedy violently asserts itself. Ed Wynn resisted this temptation. Never did he, with words, gestures or vulgarity, soil his talents. All living things, in his eyes, were allowed to breathe the freshness of life.

In the face of tragedy, in the tradition of a clown and spiritual teacher—and there is a sameness, for clownship is like a monastic order, a dedication—he lightened the burden of others, though grief filled his own soul.

His dedication taught the nation to laugh, and his throne was a solitary cloud that will never be wafted in the wind.

We all loved him.

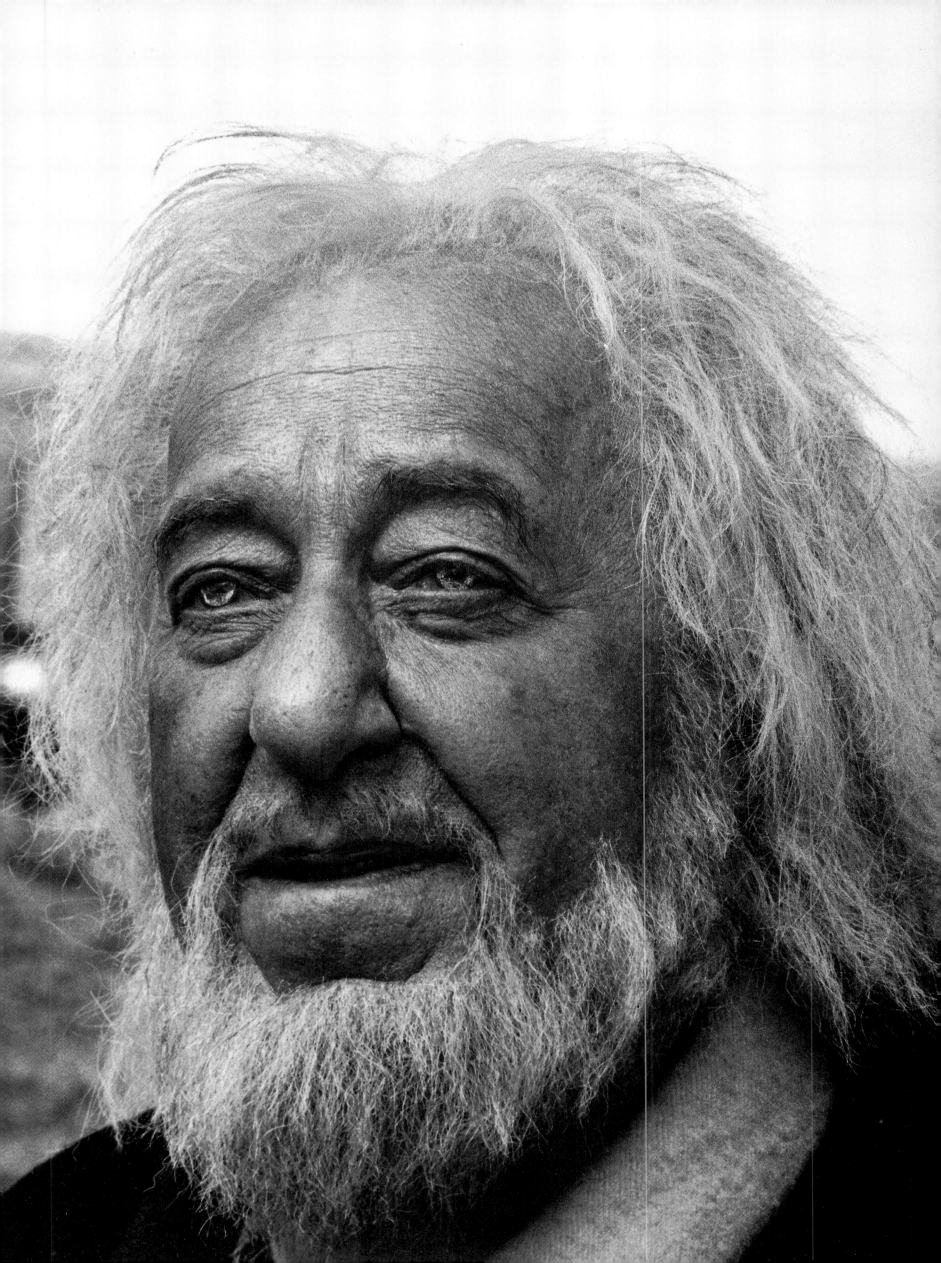

LEONTYNE PRICE
BY MARCIA DAVENPORT

Nobody knows just one Leontyne Price. And nobody knows how many Leontynes there may be. There are at least as many as the operatic roles she sings now and will yet sing. There are Leontynes of lyric and non-operatic music, and there are private and personal Leontynes whom I love perhaps best of all. I love the boisterous girl who tells a pale-blue howler in vernacular as commanding as her high C. I love the brooding, sometimes forbidding woman who inhabits the lonely place where great powers meet great works of creation and wrestle to give them realization. I love the friend who giggles with me over some feminine mischief which is nobody else's business. And I love the voice that is one of four in my lifetime which give me complete satisfaction.

What it is that voices give us is as futile to analyze as why you have fallen in love with the person you have. No other relation between a musician and an auditor is so personal. No two listeners have the same reactions to a voice. Yet a voice, however beautiful, does not make an artist. Brain and heart, discipline, intelligence, intuition, musicianship, teachability, histrionic and linguistic talents, the alchemy of personality—these turn the possessor of a voice into a singer. And these Leontyne has, along with riotous laughter, dancing feet, a dashing flair for clothes. And deep in her character, a mingling of reverence and pride, the pride you see in her swift stride when she is taking curtain calls, keeping her beaming face toward the public.

I saw it all come together a few years ago when she was singing the Verdi *Requiem* at Salzburg. The other soloists included the great mezzo-soprano Giulietta Simionato, whom Leontyne reveres and who by some chance had never sung the work in public. Mme Simionato relied rather heavily on the score she held during the performance, as soloists conventionally do. She sang superbly and so did the others. Leontyne Price sings the soprano solo of the Verdi *Requiem* with magnificence such as I have never otherwise heard, and she knows every note and word of it from the inside out. But she too held a score like the others until they had finished the *Lux Aeterna* and the mezzo, tenor and bass had sat down. Then Leontyne, alone with the concluding *Libera Me*, slipped her score onto the chair behind her and sang as is natural to her, moving much of the audience to tears.

That's *la Leonessa*. . .

JEROME ROBBINS
BY STEPHEN SONDHEIM

Jerry makes the world a stage
    (Cultivate him slowly)

Energized by antic rage
    (Hates the first rehearsal)

Runs away from saying yes
    (Optimist in chaos)

Overcomes the small success
    (Relishes Fellini)

More a poet than he thinks
    (Elegant, with giggles)

Elf and orphan, Puck and sphinx
    (Obstinate on billing)

Robbins cracks you with a look
    (Good at games and strangers)

On the stage an open book
    (Reads you in a minute)

Best of any audience
    (Amateurs explode him)

Bearded, guarded, easy, tense
    (Paradoxes make him)

In his head swim similes
    (Harrows every detail)

Never too intent to please
    (Endlessly inventive)

Sees the forest *and* the trees
    (Robbins is a genius)

OSCAR LEVANT
BY DOROTHY PARKER

EVERYBODY IS just like somebody else. It is a loathsome arrangement, but as yet, and probably as never, is anything done about it. The well-meaning, blast their souls, will break their heads trying to bring you together with your counterpart; when they succeed, and they always do, it will be as if both of you had come suddenly upon a full-length mirror, and ever after will tremble under the trauma of what you saw. Yet everyone goes right on seeking and finding replicas. Well,

42

nearly everyone, that is. The exception is Oscar Levant, which should cause no astonishment, because he is the exception to virtually everything. He doesn't even look like any other, which is one of the reasons why he is such a provocative subject for the camera.

Over years, Oscar Levant's image—that horrible word—was of a cocky young Jew who made a luxurious living by saying mean things about his best friends and occasionally playing the piano for a minute if he happened to feel like it. His stretches of illness were tossed off by the explanation, "Oh, it's just in his mind," for the speakers were of the tribe who live out their tiny lives under the persuasion that the mind is incapable of causing leaping pain. They also spread the word around that he was sorry for himself. He isn't and he never was; he never went about with a begging bowl extended for the greasy coins of pity. He is, thank heaven, not humble. He has no need to be.

Oscar Levant is a man of learning, a man of many gifts, and various not especially mysterious quirks. He is, for example, enormously superstitious; the smallest matters must be attended by elaborate ritual, and he immediately embraces any new rite as soon as he hears of it. Since he learned that Truman Capote could not endure seeing three cigarette stubs in an ashtray, he watches all such containers fiercely, so that they may be dumped before they hold the lethal

number. He is, and this can be dragged out of his most assiduous detractors, a great pianist. He is also a musicologist of the highest repute. He is free of that jealousy peculiar to artists; if he thinks someone in his own line is fine, he wishes him well, and sincerely speaks his praises. He has read, it may be said sweepingly, everything and his memory keeps it all, from the sublime to the idiotic. He has no meanness; and it is doubtful if he ever for a moment considered murder. This is not to say that there is much syrup in his make-up. In his dizziest ups and his deepest downs, he has never renounced his dislikes. They are as admirable as their targets are not. It may well be believed that the wholesome warmth of his hatreds has taken him out of his bad times, and kept him himself—and nobody else—forever.

Well. This was a losing fight before it started, this striving to say things about Oscar Levant. He long ago said everything about everything—and what Oscar Levant has said, *stays* said.

JUDY HOLLIDAY
BY GEORGE CUKOR

I FIRST SAW HER when she came into my office to read for a small part in a movie called *Winged Victory*. She had on an awful lot of pancake make-up and a lot of costume jewelry and she seemed rather odd to me. I gave her a scene to read for me. It was a very serious scene and she read it so brilliantly that I said to her, "Can you do that over again? Can you always do that? Can you do that at will?" She nodded yes. And she could, too. She had the gift that very few actresses have—you had the feeling that she'd never spoken aloud before and you had better catch it at that moment and you'd never hear it again. It was a very rare quality.

Her great success came years later, of course, with the stunning creation of Billie Dawn in *Born Yesterday*. It needs no repeating that she was a very funny girl, but like all great, great comediennes she had the gift of suddenly touching your heart. That's what made her unique, the extraordinary combination of humor and pathos. In the movies she made it always seemed the main character was based on the "dumb blonde" cliché. But under the mysterious magic of her alchemy what emerged on the screen was a distinct human being, funny to be sure, but also real and touching. And this was because she was that rarity among actresses—an artist. There are a lot of very talented people and there are a lot of instinctive people and there are a lot of clever people. But it was very rare what she had, the combination of artistry and talent and intelligence. And she had lovely looks, a marvelous face. Katharine Hepburn once said she looked like a Renoir. And she did.

She was a strange, touching girl. Odd at times, I thought, but very open and flexible and blessed with a sweet charm and sensitivity, and, above all, she had what only the best of human beings mysteriously possess. She had the grace of dignity.

RED SKELTON
BY ED WYNN

YEARS AND YEARS AGO, when I was touring with a show and we were playing for the evening in Vincennes, Indiana, I met a youngster of eight or nine selling newspapers in front of the theatre. I got to talking to him and found out that he was determined to see the show that night. Why? I asked. Because there's a great comedian from New York City named Ed Wynn playing there, he said. Well, I said, I know the manager of the theatre and I'll see that you get a seat. Later, backstage, he discovered that the fellow who had bought his newspapers and got him a seat for the show was the same fellow he had just seen on the stage. He got very excited and blurted out that he was going to grow up and be an actor too. And when I asked him what kind of an actor, he said, Funny, like you.

And he did, of course. His success and the joy he has given to the world do not have to be repeated here. But one day in 1956 that boy from Vincennes, Indiana, and that actor from New York City met again under very different circumstances. He was the star of his own television show and I was about to make my dramatic acting debut. Only I was scared. I was scared because it was something I had never done before, because I was doing very badly, and because they wanted to fire me. And as I sat there alone in a parking lot, as low as I've ever been in my life, this boy, this man I had known for so long, took me into his dressing room away from all the pressures and talked to me. He encouraged me and gave me confidence and brought me up from the ground, and after that it was all right and I was all right, and I entered upon a new phase of my career.

We all know and have enjoyed the public side of Red Skelton. He can say almost anything and make people laugh, but he doesn't need words to be funny. His humor depends on nothing but himself and his antic imagination and his great heart and dedication to do nothing more or less than to make people laugh. And to this extent he has succeeded as very few others ever have. He belongs to a very old and very honorable tradition, and its true survivors and practitioners can be counted on the fingers of one hand. He is, quite simply and quite wonderfully, a clown. He only exists to make people happy, and there are millions of people who are happy because he exists.

But to me it is the private side of this man and his incredible generosity of spirit that make me count myself blessed to know him and love him and consider myself his friend.

BARBRA STREISAND
BY JEROME ROBBINS

Barbra: some notes

CONSIDER HER: A tug-of-war goes on in all departments.

The kook's looks are ravishing. Her beauty astounds, composed of impossibly unconventional features. Her movements are wildly bizarre and completely elegant. Her body is full of gawky angles and senuous curves. It scrunches, elongates and turns on in spotlights. Her El Greco hands have studied Siamese dancing and observed the antennae of insects. She flings gestures about, sprinkling the air with outrageous patterns, but every movement is a totally accurate composition in space.

Her cool is as strong as her passion. The child is also the woman. The first you want to protect; the second, keep. She comes on with defiant independence, yet communicates an urgent need for both admiration and approval. She laughs at sexiness. She is sexy. She tests you with childish stubbornness, impetuosity and conceit, concedes you are right without admission, and balances all with her generous artistry and grace. Fighting is fun; losing, a camp; winning, the best.

51

AT REHEARSAL: An untiring, tenacious worker

She is jet-fueled with the robust, all-daring energy of an ambitious theatre novice, tempered by the taste, instinct and delicacy of a sensitive theatre veteran. At rehearsals she often arrives late, haphazardly dressed in no-nonsense clothes, her hair shoved up under a cap. She accepts the twelve pages of new material to go in that evening's performance and pores over them while schnorring part of your sandwich and someone else's Coke. She reads, and like an instantaneous translator she calculates how all the myriad changes will affect the emotional and physical patterns, blocking, costumes, exits and entrances, etc. When she finishes reading her reactions are immediate and violent—loving or hating them—and she will not change her mind. Not that day. During the rehearsal, in her untidy, exploratory, meteoric fashion, she goes 'way out, never afraid to let herself go anywhere or try anything. Nor can she be pinned down. And in the few hours' rehearsal she has probed into and examined what she must *do*, but what will *happen* on stage is being studied behind her eyes and in her nerves. That night on stage, in place of the messy, grubby girl, a sorceress sails through every change without hesitation, leaving wallowing fellow players in her wake.

52

BARBRA STREISAND
BY JEROME ROBBINS

O N S T A G E : Witchcraft.

She always surprises. Her performances astound, arouse, fulfill. When she sings she is as honest and frighteningly direct with her feelings as if one time she was, is or will be in bed with you. The satisfaction she gives also leaves one with terrible and pleasurable hunger. For what will become of this woman? She is still unfinished. Where will she go and what will she do? With all her talent and radiance, glamour, uniqueness, passion and wit and spontaneity, she is still forming. There is more to come, things will change, something will happen. The next is not going to be like the last; she promises more and more surprises. Thus she adds the special mystery to her already extraordinary gifts and achieves the true sign of a star. She is one of those very rare and fascinating performers who spellbind and then irresistibly pull you on to find out what will happen in the next moment, the next act, the next play.

This sphinx-enigma will change and alter—metamorphose. You will want to know her future, where her youthful talent and success will take her and what her life will become. She will tell. She is alike on and off the stage.

CHRISTOPHER PLUMMER
BY TYRONE GUTHRIE

T HIS IS Christopher Plummer as Marc Antony in *Julius Caesar* at Stratford, Connecticut, a few years ago. I think the picture has "caught" rather successfully some of the characteristics of his stage personality, a rare combination of the heroic and the sardonic. I would not, I think, be inclined to cast him for cozy, comfortable, gentle characters, dear old sea captains, understanding headmasters, long-suffering, unselfish Managing Directors who end up marrying the part played by Ingrid Bergman. But he can flick the whiplash of satire and contempt; he can share a joke without galumphing winks and elephantine nudges; he knows how to make a witty line sound wise and an ordinary line sound witty.

But as for the heroic, what does it take to play the great parts? Not great stature or great physical beauty. Neither Plummer, nor Olivier, nor any of the heroic actors of our era, are of Herculean physique; and the ranks are full of beautiful dimwits, godlike until they give tongue. The heroic actor can transform a fairly ordinary physique with the aid of make-up and imagination, his own and that of the audience. He cannot, however, transform a dull voice, and no amount of artifice can conceal a dull intelligence.

If Christopher Plummer took the seat next to yours in a plane or on the subway, I don't believe your girlish (or boyish) heart would go pit-a-pat. But talk to him and it won't take you long to realize that this is a voice that would not sound amiss as Hamlet, as Benedick, or as King Henry at Agincourt. Indeed it has not sounded amiss in these parts.

I hope to hear and see him as Peer Gynt, as Harpagon, as Faust, and maybe, in a few years, as Lear. It would be nice to hear him in some modern plays as well, especially if the script essayed some flights of rhetoric more ambitious than "Was it the Monday or the Tuesday?", "After you with the salad dressing," or even "Oh shit!"

54

JEAN LOUIS
BY MARLENE DIETRICH

HIS MANY TALENTS ARE UNIQUE.

It is as easy for him to design the most elegant dress as to create the most gaudy costume if the role demands it. Designing for the screen is one of his special talents. All actresses who have taste and knowledge of costumes write his name into their film contracts.

The fame of the stage dresses he designs for me is worldwide. The delight of the audience echoes around the theatres and makes me very proud of him.

I treasure his friendship.

IRA GERSHWIN
BY ZERO MOSTEL

An aspiring word mangler once asked Lorenz Hart who was the best lyricist. He answered, "First there is Ira, then me; then nobody." Ira Gershwin has other qualities. He is the only cigar smoker my wife does not mind. Me and everyone else she minds. He is also a man who complemented the perfection of his brother's music with his own poetic perfection. His volume of lyrics is a poetic outpouring. Imagine, the entire world *sings* his poetry. He is a warm, kind and gentle man, compounded with taste—witness his fine collection of paintings and sculpture. Occasionally he selects a winner in a horse race and plays an honest game of billiards. He draws and paints with the sensitivity of an artist. He *is* an artist. If he could only cook I would marry him.

THE FACE COULD LAUNCH two
thousand ships. But the quality that shines
through this particular combination of
features is perhaps even rarer—a quality
of femininity that, at its best, is intuition:
keen, direct, sympathetic, and absolutely
real. Evident at diverse moments, it is, of
course, very difficult to put into words. It
is there, though, when she is playing with
children and animals. There suddenly
through the eyes, after the first defensive
glance that may be aloof, blank, or quiz-
zical at a stranger. There in that mysterious
rapport a star of full stature seems able to
communicate through the camera's eye to
invisible millions.

ELIZABETH TAYLOR
BY IRENE SHARAFF

IGOR STRAVINSKY
BY GODDARD LIEBERSON

IGOR STRAVINSKY is a great man. You probably think me simple-minded to make such an obvious statement, because you know he is the greatest living composer.

§ I know that, too, and I accept that, but I said he was a great man.

§ It is easier to be a great composer than to be a great man. The two sometimes go together and sometimes don't.

§ If there were a church for Art, Stravinsky would be a saint. A thorny saint, but a saint.

§ As a worshiper in the church of Art, he hates the devil and fights him wherever he finds him.

§ Frequently, the devil turns out to be someone who is against Stravinsky and his music. But that would be the case with the devil, wouldn't it, if Stravinsky is a saint?

§ Everything he says is intelligent. Some of it is extremely witty, a great deal of it is acerbic.

§ I believe he would give up his sainthood if he were expected to suffer fools. But you can hardly blame him for that since he is now more than eighty years old, and he really hasn't time to do much proselytizing these days.

§ Fools will have to find out for themselves about his art and come to him later. Even if it will be when he's not around.

§ There is a story told of something that happened to Stravinsky at a dinner party. There are many of these stories and I don't know for certain if this one is true.

§ But it sounds as if it is:

§ A lady sitting next to him is supposed to have said, "Mr. Stravinsky, I just love your music. And of all your works, my favorite is *Scheherazade*."

§ At these moments the saint does not seem friendly.

§ Stravinsky turned to the lady and said dourly, "I did not write *Scheherazade*."

§ Whereupon the lady said, "Oh, Mr. Stravinsky, don't be modest."

§ He accepted that as a maxim.

§ He has never been modest since.

§ He should not be.

62

ELAINE MAY
BY MIKE NICHOLS

ELAINE MAY, as many people know, is a matronly woman in her late fifties. She is also a beautiful young starlet whose lips would be moist even if you woke her up at two o'clock in the morning. Elaine May, for that matter, is the machinelike telephone operator, the bored and coldhearted admissions nurse in a hospital and many other people you and I know very well. And when she is these people, she doesn't kid around, she really *is* them. Now here's the funny thing. How, you will ask, does she manage to let us know, while we're laughing, that the callous and robotlike telephone operator cries in the night? How come we're aware that the gorgeous and dopey starlet hasn't got a date? How is it possible that the kvetching and martyred mother, so like your mother when you haven't called for a while, should turn out to be a woman of considerable courage?

I am the logical person to answer these questions, since I have been working with and learning from Elaine for some fifteen years. Well, I'm sorry, but I have to tell you I don't know. This quality of being many different people is possessed by a girl who, as a friend, is always the same.

Richard Burton once said in public: "Elaine May is the most fascinating, maddening girl I have ever met. And I hope I never see her again." Maureen Stapleton once said in private that she is the best actress in America. When I first met her she was the most successful salesman of roofing and siding in the history of the South Side of Chicago. She burst onto the academic scene at the University of Chicago by walking into a graduate seminar in philosophy and proving to everyone's satisfaction that all the characters in Plato's *Symposium* were drunk. She was always a girl difficult to ignore.

You know how they're always saying (mostly in anthologies by Bennett Cerf) that if you have such and such a Hungarian for a friend, you don't need any enemies? Well, if you're lucky enough to have Elaine for a friend, you don't much care whether you have enemies or not.

JOHN GIELGUD
BY PETER SHAFFER

JOHN GIELGUD is the Greatest. The hip word is exact: not an adjective, but a title hardly won. It means Lord of the Game. Silver-throated Eminence. Emperor of Sound and Syllable. Potentate of the Pentameter. It describes, in the jealous and worshipful Guild of Actors, your crowned and final Mastersinger: an Imperial Wizard in a day when imperialness, even of the soul, is suspect as undemocratic—and wizardry is outlawed by incompetent magicians because they can't manage their craft.

Everyone in the theatre imitates Sir John. It is, hopefully, a way of claiming kinship with nobility. Even to be the target of one of his *faux pas* is held to establish you as a person of consequence—and God knows there are enough of them! True aficionados take a special pleasure in reciting ten of his hardest-dropped bricks in ritual catalogue, like the naming of sons in the Book of Chronicles. But always, whenever these recitals occur, one thing emerges as well: the clear innocence of their perpetrator. He is not only a stranger to malice; he is shocked by it.

Physically, J. G. is easy to do. Appearance: tall, turned-out, cuffed. Head: a cameleopard, that haughty, mythical beast off the Venetian church porch he admires. Nose: a door knocker. Eyes: vulnerable, perpetually screwed against a cigarette clenched coughingly in the lips. Walk: stiff, very swift, on the balls of the feet; a movement done always to the caption, "It is offended. See, it stalks away!" Voice: a settling foam of sound in the wake of that stalking, the only quality you really need to capture him—the golden babble, the famous high-pitched Gielgudian sackbut with its shivering tremolo and straining moments. Almost no one can resist having a go at the Voice—and almost no one really succeeds.

Listen carefully to that sound, and note what it expresses: gossip, certainly, and a cataract of opinions as glibly dropped as adopted—but something else, too: a surprising exactness, a precision of observation palpably self-coined. Many people are familiar with artificiality disguised as sincerity; it is a staple of city manners. But few will recognize the opposite—yet that is all of Sir John's secret.

The contradiction holds right through. He is an apparent Puritan, but a real sensualist. A diner off damask, but a preferer of scrambled egg. A private Romantic but a public Classicist. An extreme introvert who yet contrives to poke above the waves of his own self-absorption a powerful periscope, trained more or less exactly on other people. He is an instinctively practical man, whom breeding and biology have framed as an intellectual. In one phrase: he is the Common Man got up as a Toff.

Here, ultimately, is the secret of his pre-eminence. Obscurity does not allure him. He has the great performer's absolute need to simplify. "In a long run," he says, "you discard half of what you begin with." This is perhaps why his acting defines Classicism for me. It is like a windowpane between me and the text, so clear and light that I rarely notice how hard the words must be on the page, or how knotty their meaning is. All his great creations—the lusts of Hamlet and Angelo; the possessive fury of Leontes; his manly Cassius or narcissistic Richard—all are cut onto the glass with the same unwavering diamond—simply, surely, in a bright flowing line from which all fuss and uncertain art have been eliminated.

We all love gossip about actors' business. "So-and-so entered with a rose; so-and-so fell backwards down a flight of stairs; A. gnawed his lips or stuttered on a word; B. winked here, burped there, or was wrapped in a bear rug and thrown into the wings." No such stories will ever be told about Gielgud. He does not need them. Because his characters are Shakespeare's, not A.'s or B.'s: they exist largely in words. This is why I adore him. What you recollect of him is not gestures, gyrations, gimmicks or gallivanting. It is merely: "Ever till now,

When men were fond I smiled and wondered how" and "O that I were a mockery king of snow" and "To deal plainly I fear I am not in my perfect mind," and, for me, this above them all—standing in a blue robe which no one else in the world could wear with such authority, before the curtains of a packed house in Drury Lane at the last night of *The Tempest*:

> And my ending is despair
> Unless I be reliev'd by prayer,
> Which pierces so that it assaults
> Mercy itself and frees all faults.
> As you from crimes would pardon'd be,
> Let your indulgence set me free.

It is text. The word made flesh; made marvel; made bells and gongs; made morning light.

The theatre is like a Moroccan city. From a distance it appears white, serene, inviolable. Nearer, its streets are seen to be infested with beggars, the sad and lunatic Orders of Art: the Self-Deluded; the Self-Obsessed; the Self-Indulgent; and worst of all, the Self-Maimed, endlessly thrusting their emotional stumps at you for charity, showing their scars, or hawking their spiritual cancer as Cure. Through this clamorous throng moves Sir John, isolated by his own magnificence: a priest of precision in a world which holds that evidence of superficiality; a tragedian in an art which rejects tragedy and embraces neurosis; a musician in a barnyard. Yet these virtues will frank his passport to Parnassus, at whose foothill barrier are still inscribed the ancient, inescapable legends: *Feeling Is Not Enough* and *Phrase Is the Beginning of Praise*.

Onward he stalks in his laurels: the truest; the tautest; the sweetest; the most exact. The Greatest.

FRANCO CORELLI
BY GIOVANNI MARTINELLI

H E BRINGS BACK my youth to me. Like him, I learned how to sing by singing, and I studied much more after setting foot on the stage. It was at the Teatro Donizetti in Bergamo that I first heard him—singing Manrico in *Il Trovatore*. I remember the tremendous thrust of the voice soaring in "Di Quella Pira." He was only a youth, but I recognized the rare, true timbre of the classical tenor. And he is twice blessed because his voice can melt with lyric softness and exult with dark, dramatic power. It has the color and the ring of burnished bronze. Corelli sings and I can taste and smell Italy.

RUTH GORDON
BY THORNTON WILDER

Y EARS AGO, in the early Thirties, a friend of mine, hearing that I had been invited to give a series of lectures at the University of Hawaii, gave me a letter of introduction to her father, who was living in Honolulu, and asked me to call on him. She explained that he had spent the early part of his life as a seaman and had been around the world many times, but when he married he came ashore, found employment as a supervisor in a factory near Boston, and raised a family. Finally, having lost his wife, he had chosen to end his days on the Islands. His name was Captain Clinton Jones.

In Honolulu I wrote him, enclosing his daughter's letter, and was invited to call. Captain Jones lived in a bungalow, trig and spotless as a ship. He was in his late sixties, friendly, yet as a New Englander taciturn and as a sea captain serenely authoritative. The conversation was sedate. I was being put to a test. At last he rose, saying he had something to show me. He went to the cupboard and lifted down a large book wrapped—as this sort of book so often was—

in a great scarf, the four corners tied into a knot. He opened it and there on the front page, in the beautiful calligraphy of an earlier generation, were the words:

THE LOG OF RUTH GORDON JONES

ON HER VOYAGE THROUGH THE WORLD

Here were the press clippings that reported his daughter's career. It began with her first performance on any stage when Alexander Woollcott in *The New York Times* singled her out for commendation from among the "lost boys" in one of Maude Adams's revivals of *Peter Pan*. There were accounts of her early rise to the ranks of leading lady in Maxwell Anderson's *Saturday's Children*. Captain Jones did not live to paste into the log the glowing tributes to her performance in *Hotel Universe*, in *Serena Blandish*, in *The Country Wife* (an American girl dared to play a leading role in the Old Vic in London; the success was so great that the inflexible Miss Baylis broke the rules of her house and extended the run beyond all precedent), and in so many others.

Ruth Gordon has herself given us a full-length portrait of her father—under his own name— in what must surely be the most explicitly autobiographical play ever written, *Years Ago*—a role superbly played on stage and screen by Fredric March and Spencer Tracy, respectively.

74

One is not the daughter of a New England sea captain for nothing. Miss Gordon played the role of Dolly Levi in *The Matchmaker* over a thousand times and *never missed a performance*. More than that: before the curtain rose she was already in her chair behind the set and did not leave it during the acts except to enter on the scene. It was understood that no one spoke to her. Captain Jones must have been a notable skipper; he would do all that he was able to bring his ship and crew safely and happily to port. Leonardo da Vinci said that the essence of art consisted of an *ostinato rigore*.

Recent theatregoers think of Miss Gordon as primarily an incomparable *comedienne*. They were unable to see her in *They Shall Not Die*, a play based on the Scottsboro case, in which she gave an overwhelming picture of a vagrant Southern girl's piteous struggle To Tell the Truth, though brow-beaten, threatened and crushed. Who that saw it will forget the emotional power of her performance in *Ethan Frome*? Who can forget Mattie's *dropping and breaking Zenobia's plate*? Wide range in an artist's work does not merely denote an ability to convey strong emotion on the one hand and wit and charm and satirical observation on the other; it enriches the comedy with depth and brings a realistic immediacy to Tragedy.

Ruth Gordon's "Voyage Through the World" continues, brilliantly fulfilling the hopes of the captain who, in perfect alignment, pasted that first clipping in the' log.

When he was a boy, he used to walk up the steps to his ballet school backward, with a baseball glove and bat in his hand, in case one of his friends would pass by. He made his mother dry his practice clothes indoors and not on the windy line outside. But then he became a man; he took his career by the reins and soared to victory. Onstage he is a great dancer, a hero, a prince, romantic, flashing, dashing, smashing, a bullfighter, a panther, an actor, a heartbreaker. Offstage he is dedicated, modest, warm, giggly and a beer drinker. But best of all, he is a close friend.

EDWARD VILLELLA
BY SYBIL CHRISTOPHER

TENNESSEE WILLIAMS
BY GORE VIDAL

I LIKE NEW YORK in the summer when all the . . . uh . . . superfluous people are off the streets." The pale-blue eyes glittered, the blond moustache bristled, the loud laugh began: "heh-heh-heh," each "heh" equally stressed. Pure dactyl. That is my first memory of Tennessee Williams. Spring 1948. At a party in Rome. His first trip to Europe since the war. Mine, too. We became friends, largely because the same things made us laugh. Driving from Rome to Naples in a jeep, we invented several imaginary characters whose exploits we gravely recounted to one another. Particularly memorable was the hazardous and vicious journey of one Lesbia Ghoul to Outre-Mer, where . . . But my lips are sealed.

Other scenes: Tennessee at his typewriter in the morning. Empty coffee cup with cigarette butts stubbed out in the saucer. Through the noise of typewriter rattling, he suddenly gasps with tension as one of his characters confronts hard truth.

Forty-second Street. Midnight. One of his plays has just opened. He buys the morning newspapers. The reviews are bad. A wince of pain. Then the laugh. Then into character, an orotund creation we both affect from time to time. "You see me in my hour of travail. We shall not read the afternoon notices."

A triumphant telephone call to advise me that Governor Earl Long of Louisiana has been carried off to the madhouse. "It would seem that your comment that the political boss in *Sweet Bird of Youth* was 'incredible' was not justified. These governors are all mad as hatters. I have an instinct about these things."

A long friendship with many hiatuses. Few quarrels. I am sharp; he is oblique; we complement one another as friends ought. After reading a short story of mine, he shook his head sadly. "You are too diffident in your effects, too understated." Anticipating counterattack, he added quickly, "Now of course I tend to be somewhat overboard." He grinned. "Just think, if we were combined in one person, what a great writer we'd be!"

As he is, he is the best playwright the United States has produced. And though from time to time the fashion goes against him, he is still there, at work, making a world like no other; and we are all fortunate to have lived in his time.

TERENCE RATTIGAN
BY VIVIEN LEIGH

THIS PORTRAIT of my friend is one I have not seen. I look forward to it with interest. What aspect of Terence Rattigan has been captured? Is it Flight Lieutenant Rattigan the air gunner? Is it Terence Rattigan the justly honored playwright? Has it the gambler's gleam, the reveler's glint? Can you see the serious mien of the man who has read, experienced and knows? Of the man who has shared all this with us, not only in his writings, by which he will live, but in his daily generous actions, by which he does?

I cannot say, of course; but I can be fairly sure that it doesn't show Terry as he so often and happily leaps into my mind's eye. I see that elegant figure crumpled up with schoolboy hilarity, wiping tears of uncontrollable laughter from his eyes—laughter more often than not prompted by one of his own wicked sallies.

What I hope is that it portrays the effervescent, warm and openhearted companion that I know and love.

GIULIETTA MASINA
BY FEDERICO FELLINI

I HAVE ALWAYS considered my meeting Giulietta as predestined. Not just because she is an actress in tune with my moods and because my taste is personified in her face, her bearing, her expression, but because when we first met (she was interpreting for the radio some scenes I had written) it was as if the meeting were a confirmation of something that had always been. The rapport between us existed already, had always existed. As an actress Giulietta is a mimic, she clowns, with a light touch for every changing cadence. But she is also a rather mysterious person who becomes for me a melting nostalgia of innocence and perfection.

Naturally my life with Giulietta has been a continual fount of observation, but I don't think I have ever worked with her from motives of necessity or opportunism. Although *Giulietta degli Spiriti* was conceived of her and for her, its gestation took many years.

In every film we have made, Giulietta has rebelled against the character I offered her; she

submits only after a prolonged resistance, almost as if she were warning me against giving life to something dark, obscure, hidden within her, something she has already refuted. Alongside the enthusiastic Giulietta, the hard-working collaborator, appears the Giulietta who loathes the clothes, the look, the feel of the character and is compelled to say "no" to it all.

I think that the character who resembles her most, objectively, is this last one. At first it was a problem for me, thinking of Gelsomina and Cabiria, to distill the essence of Giulietta the woman. Then one day I discovered something. Giulietta's resistance to the make-up, the clothes, the wig, which had always seemed to me a crime against the character, intolerable feminine interpolations, this time was not only justified but necessary. My anger was out of place because for the Giulietta of this film it was right that she should take these attitudes, feel this aggression. Watching her rebellion, I saw the character emerge.

From then on, from my point of view, it was easy. There was the most tremendous collabo-

ration between us, and many times I would spontaneously ask her, "What would you do?" or "What would you say?" and then accept the answer without any modification.

On the set I am more nervous, more demanding with Giulietta than with others. I want her to be perfect instantly. I feel her as a part of me; it seems to me that she has no right to make a mistake. Sometimes I want to say to her, "But you were conceived in this story long before anyone else. How can you possibly not already be integrated in the perfection of the image we are making?"

In spite of her rebellion, her aggression and her firm convictions, in front of the camera Giulietta has a docility, a complete obedience, a total desire to make everything easy for me. But even on the set she never stops being my wife. In the midst of the arguments, the discussions, the hopes and despair, what she chiefly wants to know is whether I am cold, if my shoes are wet or if I want a coffee.

HEDDA HOPPER
BY MARY MARTIN

T HAT EYE WAS on this sparrow for many a year.

Goodness! How much the eye mirrors the soul. Certainly this eye revealed the soul of the Hedda Hopper I knew.

A lived-to-the-hilt face.

A seeing eye—filled with compassion.

A mixture of wanting to know all the facts of lives and being disappointed when they did not live up to her tremendous standards.

I knew. She had been my son's unpaid baby sitter.

A kind, tough, wonderful, innately sensitive woman who always had my admiration, my gratitude and my love.

PHIL SILVERS
BY DAVID MERRICK

I THINK PHIL SILVERS is an even greater comedian
than Jackie Gleason. Come to think of it, he is
far better than Jackie Gleason. On third thought I
believe he is the world's greatest comedian because
his comedy has such humility. It is ingenuous and
he has constantly the look of a frightened faun.

CYRIL RITCHARD
BY SUMNER LOCKE ELLIOTT

H<small>E IS THERE</small> before you see him, making his entrance with the quick, graceful movements of the dancer and the athlete. He has taken you by surprise—the tall, light walk, head erect and slightly to one side, wearing a look of slightly pained surprise, already exasperated with the situation (the tie that will not tie) taking place in the false drawing room. Then, with perfect co-ordination, feet stopping on exactly the right spot, the line is delivered with the precision of an arrow.

He greets you off stage with the same astringent affability, the same rapid, mercurial but somewhat rueful charm. He briefs you on the current situation, because something amusing and awful has always just happened or been said, and, because he is king of the wry, he invites you to share in his delight and outrage. The eyes glint with wicked enjoyment or fill with mock despair, the hands outline the situation with comic distress, the words fly out in sparks of lightning description, and you are there, you see it too, you laugh.

This lightness of the heart deserts him in rehearsal. He becomes a brooder, a worrier, subject to gloom (or what he calls "blood behind eyes"), nervously edging around a line he is suspicious of. But is it *funny*? Then "What we will need here is a *roar*, and this, I'm afraid, will only get a titterette." Yet when others quail he is captain of calm, reassuring them of their ability and quick to deal with tempests in teapots. He said once, after listening to the querulous and tearful resignation of two young song writers from a revue he was directing, "You're both absolutely right, and now sit down and have a splendid lunch and we'll discuss the first-act finale."

As director, he is everywhere, a chameleon of a comedian, taking on the shapes and colors of other characters, shaking the scene upside down to find what is in it, regarding fishily the obvious, and merciless with the fraudulent.

Nothing delights him more than the witty point well made. The exclamation mark and the exclamation mark to him, himself, was his late wife, Madge Elliott, with whom he co-starred for many years in London and in their native Australia. Madge (or "Maddie"), beautiful and apparently vague, seemingly not listening, so often made the point. Once, expostulating on his current travails out of town, on the blackheartedness and guile and feuding taking place all around him, he was heard to groan aloud that, "Oh, I couldn't survive all this horror if it weren't for the Ritz, an absolutely superb martini and Maddie," "Oh," said Madge, vaguely applying lipstick, "what terrible *billing*!"

KIM STANLEY
BY ARTHUR LAURENTS

IF SHE WANTED TO, she could be beautiful. If she wanted to, she could be a movie star. If she wanted to, she could be acknowledged the finest actress in the country. She says she wants to retire, that she acts only because she needs money. Her last Broadway appearance was in Chekhov's *The Three Sisters* under the direction of her old acting teacher.

At the moment, she has more imitators than Brando; and two are movie stars, at the moment. Perhaps her imitators reveal the point where technique becomes mannerism, but her laugh is inimitable: as unexpected as her choice of emphasis in a line of dialogue, that laugh is hoop-skirted lustiness which makes an audience beam as it reaches for a handkerchief. Nor can any imitator achieve the basis of her acting: concentration. Hers is more intense and more effectively intense than that of any other actor on the English-speaking stage. Also, no actor, imitator or not, can match her for the number of performances missed during a run, even a short run.

Some years back she asked a playwright to be patient with her, saying she worked slowly but would get all the laughs she knew were vital to her character and to the play within two weeks. She told him that the night before the New York opening. She has never been less than wonderful on live television.

A flimsy director who treated her as the frail High Priestess of the Method was nonetheless driven to desperation by her method of rehearsal and sought aid from her then analyst. "Be as rough with her as you want," he was told. "She can lick you *and* the producer *and* the play-wright with one hand tied behind her back." Another director treated her as a tigress. She rehearsed with a purr and gave a brilliant performance.

She rarely appears at a party. Once, however, when she was preparing for a divorce and an enormously demanding role, she suddenly loomed through cocktail smoke like an avenging witch. All in black from stiletto heels to an enormous circular buzz saw of a hat, her eyes were bullets and her cracks were deadly in their humor, their accuracy, and their effect on the party.

At another party, when she had just married again and was neither working nor contemplating work, she wore soft yellow. Her always incredible skin was a light golden tan that matched her hair. Even were you foolish enough not to be looking at her, you would have known from the sound of her voice that her smile was pure pleasure. But it was the endlessly kind welcome in her eyes that prompted tears. Anyone would have run off with her then and there, but no one could break through the ring around her formed by her children, her husband and, like Hamlet, by her ghost.

92

LAURENCE OLIVIER
BY NOËL COWARD

I BELIEVE Laurence Olivier to be the greatest actor of our time. Although I have no intention of qualifying this statement. I am prepared to explain, briefly, my reasons for making it.

During the Thirties I directed him in three plays: *Private Lives*, *Theatre Royal* (the English production of Edna Ferber's and George Kaufman's *The Royal Family*) and *Biography* by S. N. Behrman. In those, his young days, he was trying his wings, and never once did he flap them vulgarly. To me, vulgarity in the theatre does not necessarily mean four-letter words or slapstick —it means overacting, striving for illegitimate laughs, and not playing true.

I have seen Larry being outrageous in the theatre. His performance, for instance, of Sergius in *Arms and the Man* was a most hilarious and almost disgraceful bit of play stealing, but curiously enough it somehow was not overacting. It stayed within his own (admittedly widely stretched) conception of the part. His Mr. Puff in *The Critic* and his Captain Brazen in *The Recruiting Officer* were both pure masterpieces of farcical playing. As Malvolio his assumption of pompous, seedy grandeur, his agonizingly refined Cockney accent and his ultimate pathos will never leave my memory.

Now I should like to mention two of the parts he has played which were neither specifically comic nor tragic, but quiet, psychological studies which lie between those two extremes: Astroff in *Uncle Vanya* and Solness in *The Master Builder*. In both these divergent roles his authority, repose, subtlety and impeccable truth of characterization were beyond praise.

His greatness as a tragedian has been accepted fact now many years. His Richard III, Henry V, Macbeth and Coriolanus, to name only four, were all endowed with imagination, strength, originality and dazzling theatrical flair. His latest great classic role is Othello, and it is, to my mind,

96

one of his finest achievements yet. In the first place Othello is one of the most difficult parts ever written. It is a series of exhausting climaxes based on what has always seemd to me to be a fairly silly premise. Larry's conception of it has aroused a certain amount of controversy, the principal argument against it being that it is too Negroid. In my opinion, which perhaps need not be taken too seriously, as I am far from being a Shakespearean expert, it is this which stamps it with originality. I have seen too many "noble Moors" musically declaiming their anguished jealousy, and I have seldom been moved by any of them. In any case I am so subjugated by Larry's dedicated talent that I would fly to see him if he elected to play Hamlet as a Chinaman.

In addition to this initial genius for acting, his imagination and the meticulous concentration with which he approaches every part he plays, he has always had and still has the physical attributes of a romantic star. True, in his earlier, halcyon days at the Old Vic he made every effort to disguise these with acres and acres of nose paste and false hair. I cannot think of any other living actor who has used such quantities of spirit gum with such gleeful abandon. I believe that this rather excessive determination to be old before his time was the result of an integral shyness in his character. He has never had the smallest inclination to look or be himself on the stage. He is now the head of our English National Theatre, possibly, I suspect, at considerable financial inconvenience to himself, but definitely to the pride and honor of the profession to which he has contributed so much.

97

JANE FONDA
BY JOSÉ QUINTERO

THERE ARE SOME PEOPLE who, from the moment you meet them, you care about. Suddenly they have something to do with your life. You find yourself thinking about them at the strangest times and the oddest places. If they succeed, you succeed. If they have a failure, you have a failure. There are not many people like that. Jane Fonda is one of them.

I find myself picturing her in her house right outside Paris, almost jealous that she is married to a brilliant director. And yet the time that I spent with Jane, both professionally and socially, has been almost ridiculously short.

I suppose that people who possess this gift are bound to go into the theatre and become the myths, the symbols—in short, the truly popular and successful personalities of our time. One or two go even farther; they grow to be great actors. Jane has already achieved the first, and I have a feeling that, although not satisfied, she is working toward the other.

The first time I met her she came to read for me at the old Circle-in-the-Square for the part of Emily in *Our Town*. I had her come back twice, as I was impressed, first by her looks, which as everybody knows are quite staggering, but then I was deeply moved by her vulnerability. I did not cast her in the role: she was too individual; Emily had to be everybody. The events were the important thing in *Our Town*. With Jane we see life as it happens to her. We see it through her perspective. I think she is unafraid to see it all, and that's why I keep thinking once in a while (and I think it will become a chronic condition): What's next?

AARON COPLAND
BY HAROLD CLURMAN

W<small>HEN WE WERE</small> both still very young (back in the Twenties) I received a letter from
Aaron to the effect that he had read something in Baudelaire which would be his motto for
life. His deepest ambition, the poet had said, was to be a great man to himself. If there is
some conceit in this, there is more humility.

Aaron appreciates his own value and therefore achieves modesty without strain. This balance
is the mark of the man. In his living as in his work everything is *considered*. Aaron is the per-
sonification of *justness*: his thinking and behavior possess just measure, humane proportion. He
is profoundly serious and readily humorous. He is thoroughly intelligent though (because?) he
is no "intellectual." He is generous without being foolish, kindly without sentimentality. Being
helpful to others comes easily to him; being unaffectedly receptive to new ideas is natural to him.
He is wise and perpetually buoyant. If he had not become a composer he might have developed
into the greatest of diplomats, combining tact and forbearance with shrewdness. In all these
respects he has not changed a whit since the time he wrote me that letter.

100

ERIK BRUHN
BY VICTOR BORGE

Almost every day on TV—for a year or so—I've watched the arrival of Erik in New York harbor. It has aroused my suspicion that the great dancer commutes by Viking ship, daily, between the U.S. and his native Denmark, smuggling cigars.

If you haven't seen Erik Bruhn dance, put your imagination to work in leaps and bounds, because that's how he performs!

And a leaper he certainly is. He's leaped himself into the extraordinary rank of *premier danseur noble* with the Royal Danish Ballet (than which there is no whicher).

With his phenomenal artistry Erik Bruhn has conquered—by "see" and by "air," so to speak—two worlds. The free and the not. The sole complaint by the critics is that they want to see more of him! So, in compliance with their demand, Erik doubled his consumption of Danish butter and gained six pounds in two weeks!

This has in no way diminished his fabulous ability to (in a single leap, by Gemini!) orbit the stage with more endurance than any *Nyet-age* Russian.

It all began when Erik was a baby. His parents hired a nurse, Terpsichore Hansen, to accompany the infant in daily walks in the fresh air. So enthused was Terpsichore about the fresh air that she immediately began throwing the boy into it, higher and higher. Within a few weeks almost everybody in Copenhagen witnessed the short appearance over a rooftop or fence of a baby attached to nothing.

In no time, thanks to his inherent ability, Erik by his own power could jump even higher than the nurse was able to throw him.

When the celebrated ballet master of the Royal Theatre heard of the bouncing baby he hastily arranged an audition, which was so successful that he, the ballet master, from sheer joy, himself started jumping. Soon, joined by Erik's parents and Terpsichore, everybody was up in the air! It was a memorable sight.

Then years of hard training—the rigaudon, sarabande, gavotte, minuet. . .the tarantella, polka and the waltz. . .the fire dance, danse macabre and the dance of the hours. . .the pirouettes, entrechat, the chassé, the pas de deux, pas de trois, pâté fois gras and the Go-Go!

When I allow myself to voice such knowledge of the intricate aspects of the noble art of

102

ballet, I do so with a modest background of experience: At the age of eight—the year in which I made my debut as a concert pianist—I was put in ballet tights, though not necessarily as a result.

After my first lesson the ballet master told my father that he'd never seen anything like it and, in fact, he never saw anything like it again, for in my fourth leap I disappeared completely and never returned for further lessons.

Not so with Erik Bruhn, who faithfully continued to disobey the law of gravity. Granted, he always came down after going up, but always a good deal later than Mr. Newton had predicted. In fact, as a boy-swan in *Swan Lake* he created such a sensation that he received an offer from the local park authorities to teach the young swans in the parks of Copenhagen how, gracefully, to get up and stay there just a little longer. Erik accepted with glee and coined this timely motto: "Fly now and stay later."

The result was formidable! Not only did the birds stay up there longer, but they took off for South Africa immediately and, followed by their parents, spent the rest of their lives in the warmer climate.

Consequently there wasn't a decent swan left in any part of Copenhagen, and Erik was out of a job. He then began looking for another ballet and chose the part of Don José in the opera *Carmen*. This may appear surprising to the reader who doesn't know that *Carmen* had been transformed into a ballet for the good reason that Erik Bruhn lacked a particularly acceptable singing voice. He never could have hit the high "C," but he surely could jump it! And jump it he did, with such velocity that he catapulted his name into world fame in the press and by word of foot! His next conquest was by mistake. When his manager, who suffered from a slight speech impediment, suggested *The Sleeping Beauty*, Erik thought he said "The Leaping Beauty" and accepted spontaneously. When he awakened, the world lay clamoring at his feet, which worried him a bit because he was quite sensitive about them.

The rest is more legend.

From his triumphs as bouncing baby to incomparable *maître danseur* of the continents—from his days in the ensemble of the Royal Danish Ballet, the American Ballet Theatre and in the ballet companies from Canada to Australia—Erik Bruhn has maintained the status of exemplary *artiste suprème* and citizen, is good-looking, has a healthy appetite and 34 percent fewer cavities. Not many pianists can match that record!

A national hero, he only once had a close brush with scandal.

One cold January evening in Moscow, during the forest scene in *Swan Lake*, the electricity abruptly went off due to a power failure in Canada. Erik, at that time, was busily pursuing a couple of minor swans on loan from Yugoslavia when the lake commenced to freeze over. Slightly shivering, he hurriedly donned a pair of snowshoes and some long woolen under-drawers which his mother had knit for occasions like this. That carried him through but for a few moments when one of his snowshoes suddenly fell off and into the lake. In the process of extracting it from the freezing water his hand froze into the ice, and inadvertently he turned a cold shoulder toward the audience. Someone yelled, "Capitalist" and the curtain came down and saved the evening, which he still keeps among his souvenirs.

My father was a violinist in Copenhagen's Royal Theatre, the home of drama, opera and the Royal Danish Ballet. From my early childhood I was closely associated with these arts and many of the respective artists, some of whom became my lifelong friends, and I often had the pleasure of accompanying singers and dancers at concerts or socially. In America I have been granted the privilege of accompanying such renowned artists as Alicia Markova and Svetlana Beriosova on the stage.

But I have never met Erik Bruhn!

We both originated in Denmark and both of us are jumping all over the globe! However, not together.

My heart swells when I think of the honors he brings to our native country. And it swells when I think of the United States, who so lavishly extends her welcome and hospitality to everyone from everywhere! And my indebtedness to opportunity—who consistently has opened my door to association with so many esteemed people—is limitless, as is my gratitude to who-ever made a smile the shortest distance between two people.

I'll keep looking forward to shaking hands with Erik Bruhn. Impatiently! When he's read this article, perhaps we shall meet.

In court.

CHRISTOPHER ISHERWOOD
BY GAVIN LAMBERT

A FEW MONTHS AGO, with typical wary impatience, he said: "It's no good explaining to people why one lives here—either they understand it's the only place or they don't." *Here* isn't just southern California but a combination of vantage point and sanctuary on the rim of Santa Monica Canyon. The place is both private and accessible; the ocean is bluer and the colors are more tropical in winter than in summer—when a haze or mist tones everything down; Spanish-type houses still (just) outnumber the ugly beachheads of later architects; and enough milestones remain, human and geographical, raffish and splendid, to evoke the "great period" of a quarter of a century ago, when the bars were noisy and tacky and Salka Viertel's informal salons drew a medley of émigrés, including Garbo and Thomas Mann, Chaplin and Aldous Huxley, Brecht and Christopher himself.

Today he's the great survivor of the period and the place. Since "survivor" can imply "relic," I must point out it means the opposite in this case. I use it in the active, embattled, animating sense that Christopher is fond of using himself. "There is no question of stopping," he writes about the central character in the novel *A Single Man*. "The creature we are watching will struggle on and on until it drops. . . . It can imagine no alternative." Perhaps this explains why people often remark how young he looks and feels and is—true but not true enough, because it's only an aspect of someone who has, as they say, "found a solution." This solution is not a set of rules or exercises, *how-to* . . . hints that lead to Olympian wisdom and soothe away worry lines. It is personal, dynamic, and completely flexible except on one point. You can be tired, euphoric, depressed, in great form, drunk, dogged, like the rest of us; but there is no question of stopping. Like George in *A Single Man*, you're stuck with the future.

The most obvious connection between the legendary *Berlin Stories* and *A Single Man* is that the latter, given a little time (i.e., the future), will become equally legendary. The gift of showing people in a society at a particular vivid moment of change, the way they celebrate and squirm and walk the tightrope and wait, is uniquely his. Less obvious is a submerged link that comes at moments to the surface in *Lions and Shadows* and *Prater Violet* as well: the wry but urgent passage on fear (of age, loneliness, death, war, etc.) and what to do about it. This exposes a very personal nerve, in both senses of the word. You don't conquer it by managing not to feel it any more. You deny it at the expense of denying yourself. So? The house in which Christopher lives stands almost sheer on a high cliff. A balcony has now been added, sticking enthusiastically right out over the cliff. When you're on it, the drop down is more vertical than ever. Christopher is susceptible to vertigo and likes the balcony, just as he admires the title (as well as the rest) of a book by Alan Watts called *The Wisdom of Insecurity*. Which is a way of saying he is unsafe and sound.

EDWARD G. ROBINSON
BY LEONARD SPIGELGASS

I<small>T'S BEEN A DECADE</small> and more since he's grabbed a lapel and abjured a defenseless speakeasy owner to buy his beer, but still he's a standard for nightclub mimics, perhaps because he's The King of the Late Late Show, the quintessence of The Glory That Was Warner Brothers, the symbol of what the Thirties thought of the Twenties. The image remains constant, a classic example of the contradiction between the public man and the private man.

I've known the private man for a good long time—tough, searching, occasionally cynical, gentle, harried, an actor of range, variety and vast gifts.

But we never discuss that. Instead, we share a longing for the way eggplant used to be prepared in Bucharest (and cornmeal, too); we collaborate on speeches for so many causes all of which were and are dedicated to human dignity. For, to use a criminally tarnished phrase, Eddie is an untarnished and unabashed do-gooder, whose spirit responds to suffering instinctively, without fear of criticism or reprisal. He hates injustice as much as he loves beauty. He despises bigotry as much as he respects the theatre. He reviles insincerity as much as he worships painting.

As for that, he has collected with so rare an eye and so exquisite a touch that the walls in his home caress you. When he talks of his pictures, he's so knowledgeable and discerning that you know that something of Pissarro and Monet is in him, too. And as he goes on talking, you see that Little Caesar is so irrevocably involved in art and humanity that you'd even, if he grabbed your lapel, buy his beer.

KAY KENDALL
BY HARRY KURNITZ

IN THE WINTER OF 1951 I was traveling to England on the *Queen Elizabeth.* In those pioneer pre-stabilizer days the vessel rolled quite a lot, so the projection of the evening movie was an uncertain, wobbly affair. This one was a slight English effort, but a minor role was entrusted to an enchantress with a wildly implausible nose. I had missed the credits and my own boilers were stoked high on Dramamine, so I didn't know it then but I had fallen hopelessly and quite irretrievably in love with Kay Kendall.

A few days later in the lounge of the Connaught Hotel (time heals all things, and the movie was now completely forgotten) I came on a beautiful girl sitting alone. It was a familiar, beguiling face and I ventured a timid, hopeful "Hello." After a long look in which she seemed to be appraising my sanity she said clearly, "Move on, or I shall call the manager." And then, after considering this ultimatum, she added, "Unless, of course, you *are* the manager."

Then a third party loomed up, the man she was waiting for, Henry Cornelius, who had given her a trumpet and instant stardom in the unforgettable *Genevieve,* and we all had some drinks. She was that supreme rarity: a great beauty who was also a great, intuitive clown. Stardom affected her about as much as finding a dime would affect Nubar Gulbenkian. When her husband, Rex, was appearing in *My Fair Lady* we walked her dogs along West 52nd Street one night, and there was not a doorman or taxi driver the length and breadth of that sleazy boulevard who didn't greet her with a cheery cry, "Hi, Kay," or to whom she didn't respond with matched enthusiasm and pleasure.

In Paris much later on, when she was already quite ill, she insisted one night on being taken to dine in a Left Bank restaurant with so many strolling musicians that traffic jams and collisions with waiters made the service of food all but impossible and the noise indescribable. Nevertheless, she managed to establish communication with Rex by means of a primitive wall telephone, and I heard her shouting cheerfully, "I'm being a *very* good girl, darling. A quiet dinner and now I'm in the Christian Science Reading Room with Harry Kurnitz."

And that's how I remember her.

110

OSKAR WERNER
BY STANLEY KRAMER

IT IS PATRONIZING to appraise an artist in his time—
and overly sentimental to suggest his pedestal.

Oskar Werner is an exceptional artist. More than that,
total commitment to the integrity of his art is a way
of life. The blend of artistry and commitment—it means
so much and promises so much more.

MAUREEN STAPLETON
BY CAROL GRACE

MAUREEN STAPLETON'S superb face rests somewhere between that of a saint and a Christmas-tree angel. It has depth and aspiration, and flossy sad silent-movie-star prettiness. It is a perfect expression of her. She is the only actress I have ever seen who has the delicacy and the hurt to play Blanche du Bois and the power and the hurt, if given her to do, to play King Lear. The beautiful thing that occurs when she is on the stage is no more and no less than the translation of what she dreamed about, what she ate, what she wished for, what she forgot to do yesterday, what she bought at Porthault's and what she is going to buy at Bloomingdale's. Her acting advice is: "Get a lot of sleep and talk loud." Her housekeeping advice is: "Hose down the kitchen." Her official disaster statement is: "Sheer luck." Her description of almost anyone is: "He is perfect." One early summer evening she planned to have dinner at the most fashionable restaurant in Saratoga Springs. We'd spent the afternoon playing essences on the beach. When it was almost time to leave, I reminded her that she wasn't dressed for dinner. She was still in a beach dress. She glanced up from the book she was reading —*The Family That Slays Together Stays Together*—and said, "I'm almost ready." She then put on a string of pearls and said she was dressed. She was.

RUDOLF NUREYEV
BY LEONARD BERNSTEIN

Always the most romantic
drive in man has been his defiance of gravity;
and his most exalted acts are physical
manifestations of that drive:

The reckless upward plunge of Gothic cathedrals.
The thrust of skyscrapers, and all erections.
The free flight of airplanes, and all rockets.
Nureyev's leap into primeval light.

MARGOT FONTEYN
BY OLIVER MESSEL

I T W O U L D B E impossible for me to attempt to add to the innumerable accolades that have been written about the superb artistry of Margot Fonteyn. But since I have experienced the delight of designing ballets for such an inspiring person, what has perhaps struck me more than anything else is the way that the rare integrity of her character is projected through her every movement on stage. Her selfless dedication, superb manners and modesty, found only in the great, have placed Margot on a pedestal to be adored by everyone who is near her. By her example Margot has set the highest standard and is the inspiration for the whole ballet to follow.

The rose that Margot gave to me from her bouquet on the stage of the Metropolitan Opera House in New York at the opening performance of *The Sleeping Beauty* is one of the moments I treasure most of an unforgettable evening.

TOMMY STEELE
BY GENE KELLY

I BELONG TO A very special fraternity—it's that group that is loosely called "Song-and-Dance Men." Every once in a while we older members find a new applicant—someone we'd like to make a part of our company.

Well, this past year we've found one. His name is Tommy Steele. He sings, he hoofs, he can turn a fast quip or play a sober scene—he has all the requirements called for. But he has something else. A very *special* something else. It's that unique quality that makes an audience glow, that makes it laugh or cry but particularly makes it *love* the performer and to be glad it's there with him.

I can't tell you the why for this. I don't think anyone can. But I *can* tell you that when Tommy is on the stage—singing, dancing or playing a scene—the theatre is a joyous place.

Mr. Steele—welcome to the club!

121

JACK LEMMON
BY BILLY WILDER

HAPPINESS is discovering that your daughter is in love with an older man—Paul Getty.

Happiness is having a doctor who smokes four packs a day.

Happiness is working with Jack Lemmon.

GLADYS COOPER
BY ROBERT MORLEY

BUT SURELY I've told you this story before?" They shook their heads. "About the bears? The bears in Yosemite Park?" They pretended not to have heard it.

"Your grandmother was determined to take a picture of the bear. The bear was determined to stay in the shade. There were large notices everywhere warning people not to feed the bears. To keep away from them. Bears are treacherous, unpredictable. Stay in your cars, the notice boards advised. Your grandmother went up to the bear and smacked him smartly on the rump. 'More over, dear,' she told him. 'There's a good boy.' It was then that I wound up the car window and locked the door. I reasoned it would take me just that much longer to get to her and perhaps by then the bear would have made off.

"I closed my eyes and waited for the crunch of bear teeth on human flesh. When I looked out a little later, your grandmother was holding the camera an inch away from his nose. 'This must be the last,' she told him firmly.

"Both of them were surprised when they reached the car to find the door locked.

124

" 'Why didn't you come and help?' Gladys demanded. The bear said nothing but looked displeased. They say animals can smell terror. I thought it unwise to wind down the window. 'Get in the other side,' I begged her.

" 'But I'm driving.'

" 'Why not let the bear drive?' My voice rose shrilly. 'Don't you read notices? Why can't you ever do as you're told? They're not fools. They know more about bears than you do.'

"As we drove away the bear suddenly stood up on his hind legs. 'You see,' I told her, 'he wanted to kill you.' 'What he wanted,' said Gladys, 'was to have me take another picture of him. Who do you think knows more about bears than I do?' Everyone. I proved it years later in '21.' Your grandmother ordered trout. 'For two?' asked the waiter. 'For one,' I told him. 'I'll take the honey bear.' 'I don't believe it,' said Gladys. I showed her the menu. 'Personally,' I added, 'I don't think I could bring myself to eat trout. Poor inoffensive little

126

creatures. Give me a good hunk of bear—something I can get my teeth into before he gets his into me.'"

"The story I like best about my grandmother," one of them said, "was when she thought General Motors was a *real* general and was so annoyed that no one introduced her."

"Or the time they stole her car and the policeman asked if it contained any valuables and she said, 'Yes . . . a loaf of bread.'"

"When they stole all her jewels and none of them was insured and they asked her what she was going to do about it, all she said was 'Have another cup of coffee.'"

"But the best story about Gladys . . ." And they all started to talk at once.

The best story of Gladys Cooper should, I suppose, be the legend of her fabulous successes and occasional failures over the years in the theatre and on the screen. Her family and friends are infinitely more fortunate to have known and loved not the legend but the lady.

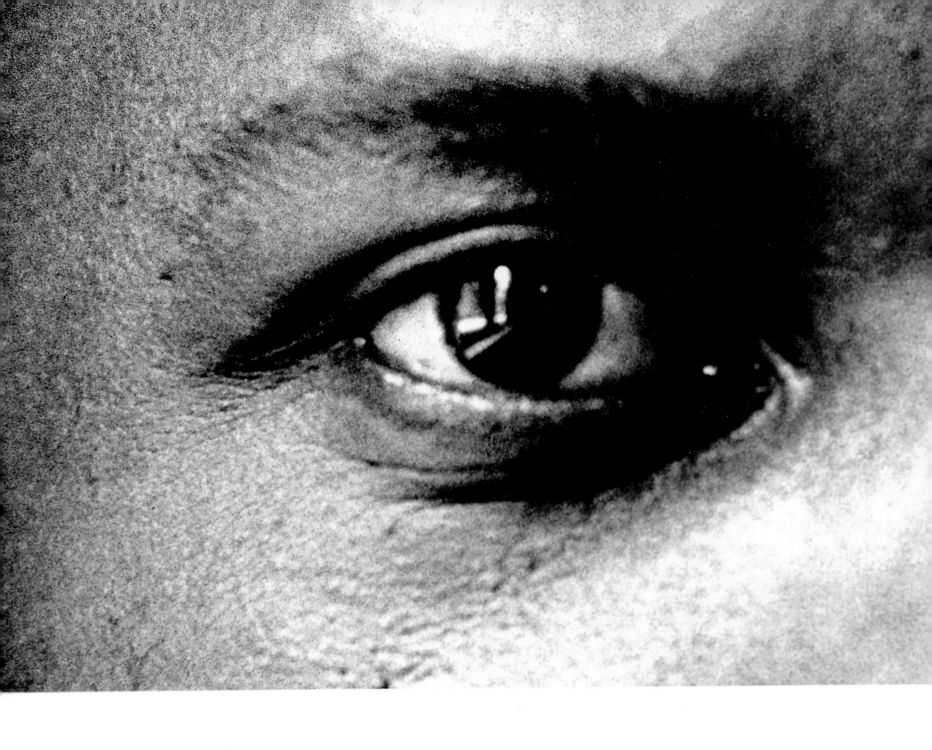

ALFRED NORTH WHITEHEAD ONCE WROTE:

"Our minds are finite yet even in these circumstances of finitude we are surrounded by possibilities that are infinite and the purpose of human life is to grasp as much as we can out of that infinitude."

This be the fuel that drives my friend, Sidney Poitier.

128

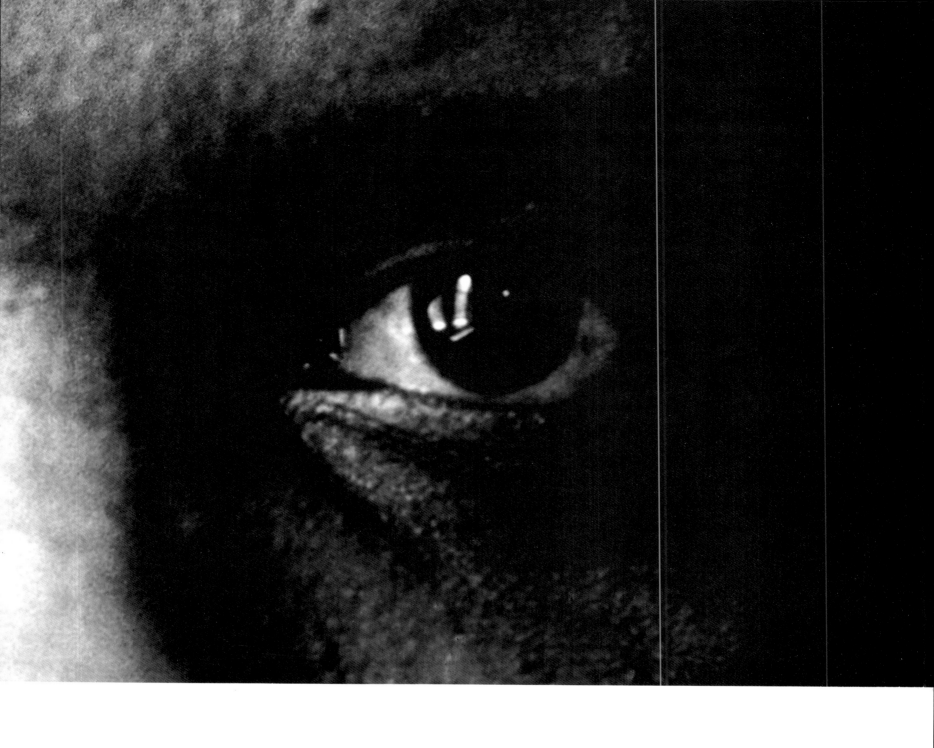

SIDNEY POITIER
BY HARRY BELAFONTE

MARY MARTIN
BY JACK PAAR

MARY MARTIN is the most natural, unspoiled actress or woman I have ever met. She can ride a horse, herd cattle, drive a truck, and still sit like a queen in a Rolls-Royce. She's equally at ease with Noël Coward or a Brazilian cowboy. She loves people: a theatre full or only a few at a church wedding in the forests of Brazil. Of course Mary also sings, dances, paints—

and we all know she can fly. She is, by any standard, one of North and South America's most valuable resources.

MICHAEL PARKS
BY HENRY FONDA

I HAVE NEVER MET MICHAEL PARKS.

A couple of years ago I turned on television to watch a show starring one of my favorite young actors—boy named Peter Fonda. Playing the other principal role in that television play was a boy who was completely unfamiliar to me.

There was something about his personality and the kind of strong yet sensitive performance he gave that made me look for his name when the credits came. It was Michael Parks.

Some time later I began to hear that name again. He was one of the most promising young movie personalities, I was told—William Inge had written a screenplay for him; John Huston had cast him as Adam in *The Bible*; he was to play opposite Kim Stanley in another movie. People whose opinion I respected spoke highly of him.

I was also surprised—but, I confess, pleased—to hear that, in an interview, he had told the reporter that he sought out pictures like *The Grapes of Wrath* and *The Ox-Bow Incident* as films he wanted to see over and over again. He had some very flattering things to say about me.

A mutual friend told me that Michael was coming to my play and asked if he could come backstage to the dressing room to meet me. The time went by and he didn't show up. Later I was told that he felt "shy and self-conscious" about the meeting. I understand that—I'm a lot like that myself.

I think he is a young actor of great talent and individuality. People say he reminds them of James Dean or the early Clift or Brando. I see what they mean. I think there is an excitement about him that is similar to the excitement those others created.

But I don't think Michael Parks is a carbon copy of anyone. He's his own man and I think he'll go far.

I hope so. You can never have too many good young actors; in these days, I worry that there may be too few. But then I remember boys like Peter Fonda; like Richard Jordan, who played with me in *Generation*; like Warren Beatty, who certainly has his own excitement; like Jim MacArthur; and a few others. And like Michael Parks. And I'm not really worried about where the good actors of the future are coming from.

MIKE NICHOLS
BY JOSEPH L. MANKIEWICZ

"**M**IKE NICHOLS" (Mīk Nĭk-ŭls): through the ages, variously, Demigod; Poltergeist of the Theatre; Dybbuk of the Performing Arts; *et al*, Capable of—and given to—materializing in human form.

Except for cloven hoof (most preval., Holy Roman Empire, *et seq.*), inability to cast shadow or produce reflection in mirror, EMEN ("M.N.")* invariably assumed uncanny likeness of most applauded, most successful theatrical artist of whatever period. Most distinctive characteristic, however, by which other (i.e., mortal) artists detected presence of EMEN amongst them: the heavy, cloying effluvium of talent which He (It) exuded to an objectionable degree.

*(n.b.: "M.N." is, of course, colloquial vulgarization of EMEN—earliest Aramaic epithet for Mīk Nĭk-ŭls. *Cf.*, in particular: *Dybbuk, Quo Vadis?* (Lantz, Stuttgart, 1933); *An Enquiry into Psychosomatic Success* (Burton, Rome, n.d.).

In mythology (Greek), at first thought to be only natural Son simultaneously conceived by Zeus of *more than one* mortal woman and born by them in unison. Later, more enduring concept (Greco-Rom., *et seq.*): EMEN as the only Son of Zeus and Mnemosyne. Thus, the enchanting inference that the nine Muses were EMEN's (Mīk Nĭk-ŭls) nine Sisters.

Only fragmentary descriptions remain (*viz: "i Mutilati"* or *Zanuck* scrolls) of the elaborate rites wherein Greek playwrights, producers and actors invoked EMEN to infuse their efforts with a Talent beyond mortal attainment. It appears that human sacrifice was rare (an occasional elderly Chorus member, at most), but almost certainly manuscripts were burned. In his *Dybbuk, Wo Bleibst Du?* (Buenos Aire, 1935), Von Preminger projects the interesting concept that many celebrated missing Greek plays were actually stolen from each other by rival playwrights, then destroyed in sacrificial invocation to MĪK NĪKŬLS—EMEN (by now).

Such rites, among others of lesser import involving religion, etc., came to an end with the advent of Christianity (De Mille, 1881-1959). Subsequently, not only was the invocation of

EMEN as Demigod and divine *urquelle* of talents theatrical forbidden, but His (Its) beneficent powers of bestowing phenomenal success upon the ordinary work of the ordinary artist were condemned as Pagan and heretic, even Satanic.

Inevitably, then, through the Dark Ages, EMEN undergoes an etymological transformation—to emerge, understandably perhaps, first as a symbol of artistic disaster in dramatic ventures—and then as full-fledged poltergeist of the Drama. Ultimately, coincident with Miracle and Morality Plays (10th–16th Cent.), MĪK NĪKŬLS–EMEN (interchangeable by now) becomes a colloquial theatrical curse. Thus, *e.g.*, one artist to another: "May your work follow a Mīk Nīkŭls!" (*i.e.*: may it appear following a tremendous success, when the panegyrics of critical and public approbation have been exhausted). Or, *e.g.*, (psych.): "EMEN has put his curse upon me!" (*i.e.*: a justification or explanation for various artistic blights suffered by creative persons such as "writer's block," "director's stupor," "actor's block-and-stupor").

S. Spiegel, in his scholarly *Dybbuk Reissued* (Panama, n.d.), documents rather successfully the ironic transformation of EMEN, beneficent Demigod of Antiquity, into MĪK NĪKŬLS, dread Poltergeist of the Middle Ages. Among the Saints most frequently invoked by the medieval artist *against* (the irony cannot be stressed too strongly) being "possessed" by MĪK NĪKŬLS, Spiegel cites: ST. FRIDOLIN, protector of spectacle-makers (can Spiegel be in error here?); ST. GENESIUS, protector of actors; ST. JUDE, of the impossible; and, significantly, one whose importance has not yet been properly probed—ST. SUBBER (canonized 1964-65).

The transitional process by which MĪK NĪKŬLS, in the course of the 17th, 18th and 19th Centuries, managed to emerge *once more* as a symbol of ecstatic gratification and limitless success in matters dramaturgical is a confused one. There is available only the most fragmentary, indeed elusive, evidence of its etymological path. Random and apparently unrelated references, for example, by both Lessing and Diderot to ". . .*ein Komiker, der sich Mike Nichols nennt*" (Lessing) and "*J'ai recontré, aujourd'hui, la* [*sic*] *Mike Nichols*" (Diderot). It is unlikely that either has any relevance to our subject.

Still, while no longer, of course, regarded as of Divine origin, the *contemporary* connotation of Mīk Nīkŭls (as a "working" phrase of common usage in our modern theatre) has come full circle, as it were, and has very nearly reacquired its earliest meaning. Today, then, Mīk Nīkŭls could be defined as, succinctly:

a) The attainment of unattainable critical and public "kudos" (Grk. orig: *Boffo*). b) A condition of unexplained and boundless euphoria which sometimes seizes an artist immediately

136

preceding the actual public presentation of his work. c) In general, the egomaniacal excesses of an artist's fantasies in contemplating his future.

Some random references and epithets relative to EMEN-MĪK NĪKŬLS perhaps worthy of hurried mention: the earliest, of course, known to every schoolboy, was His (Its) very first— "EARTHSHAKER." (Grk. antiq., *also* Greco-Rom.) An ingenious, if unsupported, connection is suggested by Kurnitz in his *Dybbuk's Dictionary* (Playboy, Oct. '00), between "EARTHSHAKER" and "SHAKE-SCENE"—the latter, a common vituperative Elizabethan theatrical epithet. Upon one reported occasion, Robert Greene, playwright—obviously invoking the curse of Mīk Nīkŭls (see above)—made use of it in a venomous attack upon another, more celebrated, actor-playwright in the Elizabethan Theatre.

Then, too, Comden and Green (Ital., 1940-) offer a provocative projection of EMEN-MĪK NĪKŬLS into the Italian Renaissance in their cryptological analysis, *Florentine Dybbuks Deciphered* (Grossinger, 1943-44). Most ingenious are their cabalistic insinuations regarding M. NICCOLÒ Machiavelli.

Another, later, area for exploration (Germ., *Strum u. Drang, et seq.*) is uncovered by Cerf in his *Dybbuk of Buks* (priv. printed, n.d.). Cerf finds significant the unique use of "Fuehrer" as appellation for enormously talented, abnormally successful German theatrical artists—whereas elsewhere in the Western World such types were more properly referred to as EMENS (Mīk Nīkŭlses). ("Fuehrer," the word, has since been vulgarized in a political sphere of reference.)

Lack of time, space and—modestly, perhaps—erudition prohibits even a definitive outline of the countless references, anecdota, influences, fictions and myths relative to, even attributed to, Mīk Nīkŭls which pervade the Theatre of the World, its Literature, its Dramaturgy, its very Being—after all, "*Le Déluge, c'est Lui,*" said Voltaire (Fr.).

The scholar, however dilettante, is confronted by them wherever he turns—even to the East. (Ustinov's [Hung., 1890–] *The Mystique of* NICHEVO is most provocative here.) In South America, too, numberless brilliant efforts, apparently without identifiable authorship, have frivolously been attributed to "ANON." Much too easy. And unacceptable. "ANON," after all, as a simple anagram for the Subject of our searchings, can be identified by any schoolboy (see above).

Further, there is only this to record: that there is no known mention or evidence, in any of Its (His) manifestations, materializations or influences, of Mike Nichols on the North American continent. We are not a superstitious people.

—J. L. MANKIEWICZ
(ALEXANDRIA, 30 A.D.)

THERE IS NO young performer today who seems less in need of analysis. Somehow, at a relatively tender age, he has managed to discover the secrets to portray successfully that rarest of mid-century heroes: the interesting non-neurotic. He acts with enormous intelligence. More than any of his peers, he gives the impression of not only having gone to college but also actually of having gotten something out of it.

He is not only gifted, he is skilled; not only skilled, but magnetic. Listening to the ladies chatter during the intermissions of *Barefoot in the Park* substantiates this last. As they praised him, one could tell they were also preparing for him some soft segment of their daydreams. Redford is here and likely to linger.

We men may just as well get used to him.

ROBERT REDFORD
BY WILLIAM GOLDMAN

BEATRICE LILLIE
BY BROOKS ATKINSON

BEATRICE LILLIE is a slight, elegant lady with sharp features, a modish personality, a small, tight, abashed grin and a genius for satirical comedy. Her manners are reserved. She does not overwhelm an audience; she conquers it with wit and intelligence. Despite her dainty and detached personality she is also a vastly entertaining low comedian. A gleam or a grimace from her is as intelligible to the audience as a slapstick. What devastates us is not so much the material as the flashes of brilliance that come from a satirical mind. It is a hard mind that hates sentimentality, hackneyed art, pretentiousness and buncombe. Miss Lillie is not part of the thing she is portraying. A little detached, she is always looking at it ironically, making fun not only of the character but of the entire organization of social life. She undermines everything she pits her mind against, for she is both a pithy actress and a caustic satirist.

OTTO PREMINGER
BY ROALD DAHL

H IS HEAD IS so big it makes him look top-heavy. From a distance, standing as I saw him one morning in the middle of a lawn above Pearl Harbor, he looked like a huge pink mushroom sprouting from the grass.

Many who do not know him intimately (but who think they do) are inclined to misjudge him seriously. They say, for example, that he is a tyrant. This is untrue, although when making a picture he often looks like one. He explodes. He yells and screams. He goes purple in the face. The whole company trembles. The heavens open and the veil of the temple is rent in twain. And when it is all over he resumes work as quietly and calmly as if nothing had happened.

I believe that Otto could control these explosions if he wished. In fact I will go further and say that he creates them purposely and uses them as psychological therapy. In much the same way as a man will induce a belch of gas to relieve the pressure in his stomach, Otto will induce a belch of words to relieve the tensions in his nervous system. He is far too intelligent to think that yelling blue murder at an actor is going to improve his performance. It never has and it never will. But when one is entirely responsible, continuously, day after day, over ten weeks,

144

for the expenditure of $100,000 a day, it is desperately important to remain relaxed and serene throughout. And that is why Otto, whenever he feels the slightest little tension building up inside him, opens the top and lets off steam until the pressure returns to normal.

He is, because of all this, probably the most relaxed man in the business. During the filming of *In Harm's Way*, a middle-aged masseuse who had been summoned to the hotel to give him a workout said to me later, "That man doesn't need a massage! He doesn't have a tense muscle in his body!"

Otto Preminger is a man of culture and intellect. He despises pretension. He is a brilliant producer and organizer. He has immense moral courage. And in the business of making motion pictures, where many come and many go every few years, he is continuously and spectacularly successful.

In private life he is warmhearted and enormously sentimental. He adores his wife and he goes quite limp with joy whenever he looks at his children. I don't blame him. It is a beautiful family.

ESTELLE WINWOOD
BY TALLULAH BANKHEAD

O F A L L T H E British actors who have been knighted in the last seventy years, from Henry Irving to Felix Aylmer, my favorite is Sir John Hare. Why? Because Sir John had the rare good sense to give fifteen-year-old Estelle Winwood, my oldest and most valued friend, the role of Laura in his revival of *School*, a comedy by T. S. Robertson, thus enabling her to face her first audience at the Theatre Royal, Manchester.

In the long interval since Estelle's first night in Manchester, none has served our theatre more faithfully or more skillfully, or with such cool detachment. Estelle is as invulnerable to the fevers of success as she is to the agues of despair. Though she's been ambushed in her share of disasters, never, to quote Henley, has she winced or cried aloud. Her serenity, however hot or cold the dice, is the envy of everyone on Equity's roster.

Throughout my professional life Estelle is the one I've turned to when shattered by the necessity of making a decision—a decision that may be freighted with weal or woe. She has never failed me. Fragile and delicate in appearance—as one critic observed, a snowflake would give her a concussion—Estelle is granite in a crisis. A world with more Winwoods would be a more desirable sphere on which to fret and fume.

ETHEL MERMAN
BY JOHN GIELGUD

THE VOICE OF Miss Merman, on radio or phonograph record, does not prepare one for the artistry with which she uses it when one first sees her on the stage, though one still delights in the confident ease with which she welds together the tune and lyrics so firmly and, as it seems, spontaneously.

Like all great comedians, she can suddenly evoke tenderness and an unexpected simplicity of expression that are strangely moving in contrast to her broad, even sometimes brassy, technique in putting over a sophisticated number. Her scene of tucking up the children in bed in *Annie Get Your Gun* was absolutely true and touching, and I shall always remember it. She presents herself uncompromisingly, without any attempt to assume false glamour. In *Gypsy* she even presented a kind of monster mother and in *Annie* a plain, awkward creature. The absolute truth of these two performances struck home immediately, as the warmth emerged so surely and gradually from behind the formidable defensiveness of the outward appearance of the characters she was portraying.

Of course, she is always Ethel Merman. That striking assurance of hers enables one to relax at once, as she comes forward and begins to sing, her black eyes sparkling as she hits the first note and swings or croons into the line of the melody—every word clear and crisp, the rhythm and flow controlled with perfect time and breathing—and, as she finishes her last note and walks off toward the wing, one sighs with satisfaction at the perfection of her technique and the apparent ease and skill with which she can take such unquestionable command of a huge audience. She needs no plumes or expensive gowns—though she can carry off such fantasies too; can be splendid, chic, vulgar or domineering if she wills. She can stand in a plain jersey and skirt and hold the house in absolute stillness so long as she cares to go on singing. Her unique qualities of magnetism and authority, the power, the selectivity, homeliness and warmth with which she takes the stage, combine to create the remarkable artist that she has made herself, and I shall always count myself as one of her very greatest admirers.

SAMUEL GOLDWYN
BY SAM SPIEGEL

For more than fifty years Samuel Goldwyn's name has been a synonym, the world over, for the best and the bravest in motion pictures. His contributions to every aspect of the medium are incalculable. A list of his productions reads like an anthology of the finest in the history of the cinema.

And for just as long his fame as a master of malapropism has added an odd sort of luster to his public image. It is a tribute to his stature that the jokes have only enhanced that image. It is a tribute to his sense of humor that he never tried to amend that image.

In a milieu where adjectives are thrown about very casually, Sam has truly earned the right to be called a giant.

Perhaps the only one left.

152

OLIVER SMITH
BY TRUMAN CAPOTE

OLIVER? Oh, Oliver *Smith*. Yes, of course I know him. Ought to. We shared a house for almost ten years—this was on Willow Street in Brooklyn Heights. Beautiful house. Oliver's still there. What do I think of him? Hmmm. Well, quite a lot of things. He's really very nice. And truly has grace under pressure. In the deranged world of theatrical endeavor, his haughty aplomb, his merely amused poise is admirable, even startling. As for his artistic self—certainly he is the most versatile stage designer any country has ever produced, and his best productions (*Fall River Legend, West Side Story, My Fair Lady, On the Town*) are as good as the best work ever done by anybody. Even so, it is my belief that Oliver chose his career unwisely. He is too intelligent and refined to be associated with the entertainment industry. He has the eyes, the hands of a great surgeon—and the precision of mind. If I were undergoing a serious operation, I should certainly want the doctor to look like Oliver—and to have his temperament: gentle, highly human, yet expertly detached.

154

HENRY FONDA
BY JOSHUA LOGAN

A S AN ACTOR, Henry Fonda is unseduceable. Once he has perfected a performance it is inviolate. Other actors, even some of the greatest, blossom or wilt when an audience blows hot or cold. Not Fonda. By the time he's etched his character, the fine lines have burnt deep and unwavering into the copper plate, and each printing is as clear and readable as the one before. There is no blurring, no paling, no double image.

I have seen him play a role for the first time and then again for the thousandth time. All around him actors were catering to adulation—that little ecstatic wiggle, the extra uncalled-for tilt of the head, the ever-so-slight peek toward the audience which says, "You and I both know how delicious I am."

We as an audience love to seduce an actor. It is not only in some way satisfying to see him or her give in; it is also perversely pleasurable to have the power to humiliate publicly, to watch the poor creature fawn or bask or preen himself. This is impossible with Fonda.

Though his performance has been conceived with passion, turmoil, gargantuan querulousness over tiny points, minutiae that seem so unimportant to the director or author who are dealing with the whole and therefore have little patience for the specific at the moment; though he has used every device known to man to find truth, to search out a character that he is able to portray

156

with abject faith, once has latched onto his "person," discovered his "person's" thought stream, mastered his emotional progressions, Fonda has distilled a kind of personal ink for the character with which he has stained himself, and this ink is of a color that will never fade.

And this color is of such a subtle tint that no other can trace the formula. If anyone should ask you, you'd say it was white, because while the lesser actors around him parade their motley in front of the whimsical audience, changing veils as though for a sultan, Fonda moves through it all as clean as Cyrano's white plume. After scores of forays he remains belligerently virginal.

And we should thank our national gods that he never had time to study voice or diction. Without that flat whine, that Nebraskan screech with which he portrays both humor and anger, without the tonelessness of the plainsman, where would our top symbol of the American be? Hidden in a cloak and doublet surely, swathed in a toga, doomed to the selflessness of the great classic actor—hidden like the purloined letter in plain view but invisible in a great repertory company.

As a hobby, Hank Fonda paints still lifes which are as *trompe-l'oeil* as his performances on the stage. You cannot see the brush strokes, but you can feel the patient dedication and be amazed at his observance of shape, shadow, reflection and texture. You would guess these detailed ar-

HENRY FONDA
BY JOSHUA LOGAN

rangements of fruit or vegetables, still dripping with water on freshly unfolded tablecloths, were painted by the great Dutch masters of the seventeenth century. These paintings might lead you to believe they were the creations of a man devoid of humor.

But Henry Fonda has another ability which is close to genius. He is a great clown. Under other circumstances he could have earned his living and perhaps even more fame than he has in a circus or with the Mack Sennetts of his time. I believe that it is lucky for Charles Chaplin, Harry Langdon, Buster Keaton and Emmett Kelly that he didn't join their game.

But Henry Fonda is no saint. If he is a religious in his profession, he is a snarling one. Don't give him an easy answer if you are director. Don't give him a false scene if you want to be a happy, healthy playwright. Don't come into town with less than a perfect play with a perfect cast or you will never hear the end of it. He has been known to give interviews in which he begged the public to stay away from the production he was playing in at the time. And above all, if you are an actor in his company don't let him catch you overplaying, turning toward the audience with a warm look, don't add an "if" or an "er" or a "but" to the script, don't slow down or speed up, don't avoid his eyes when he's playing a scene with you. Don't be seduced in front of the Great Unseduceable.

NANCY WALKER
BY PHIL SILVERS

NANCY WALKER as an actress to me epitomizes the word "professional"—a word I don't toss around loosely.

During our association in the Broadway and subsequent road tour of Garson Kanin's *Do Re Mi*, I can't honestly say I remember her varying her performance one inch. This is not to imply a certain monotony but an adherence to an attained perfection.

Off stage, Nancy is a love and a compassionate companion.

Unlike too many performers, she is in touch with the world and its happenings. I very much like Nancy Walker.

Oh—one suggestion—don't move on her lines.

160

BUSTER KEATON
BY LOUISE BROOKS

SINCE CHILDHOOD I have thought Buster Keaton's the most beautiful face of any man I have ever seen, and finally in 1962 I got an opportunity to tell him so. We were in his Sheraton Hotel suite in Rochester during the time he was making a commercial film for Kodak. I was speaking of a shot of him hiding under a table in *The General*: "You were so terribly beautiful in its tragic lighting, Buster, so out of key with your comic character—I can't understand why you didn't cut that shot out of the picture."

Although the tragic prophecy of that close-up was now visibly chiseled upon the purity of his face, he had evidently never considered people's reactions to its beauty. For an instant his expression was mystifyingly shaken up like a snowstorm in a crystal paperweight, and then, dismissing the whole damned thing, with his little-boy walk he trudged into the kitchenette to get himself a cold beer.

For it was as a little boy that he established his comic character, and he remained this same little boy until those destructive experiences known as "reality" smashed his lovely world to smithereens. Part of this world in 1928 was Buster's Beverly Hills estate, a magnificent playpen full of hilarious activity. Keaton at home was no different from Keaton in films. He went about each project with the same adorable conviction of a good little boy doing a good thing in the best possible way. After the most idiotically inspired dives off the springboard into the pool, he would go to the patio to barbecue the most perfect steaks. Indoors in the living room above a high balcony, it had pleased him to rig a red velvet curtain on which he could swing down across the room to the top of a grand piano. When, with Louis Wolheim, he played thousand-dollar bridge games against such combustible opponents as Sam Goldwyn, he was still having a grave good time, confident that he would win. And he always did.

One midnight he took a fancy to drive Buster Collier and me in his roadster to Culver City, through the gates of the M-G-M studio and out to his bungalow on the back lot. Against three walls of the sitting room were tall built-in bookcases. Buster opened the front door, flipped on the light, picked up a baseball bat and, strolling neatly around the room, smashed the glass in each and every bookcase. Who then could understand how much more terribly prophetic was this act than the close-up in *The General*? But who then could foresee that within so short a time his job, his family and his home—all would be lost to him? Thank goodness, he never lost his skill with a baseball bat.

JENNIFER JONES
BY HENRY MILLER

THANK GOD I have not yet seen *all* the films in which Jennifer Jones has starred. Had I seen nothing more than *Good Morning, Miss Dove* I would never have forgotten her. I wait for it to appear again just as I wait to see once more—or twenty times more—*Goodbye, Mr. Chips*, *Lost Horizon* and *The Informer*. No matter what the role, I wait to see Jennifer Jones, always certain of being thrilled and enchanted. To me she is like a coin fresh from the mint, whether playing the angel, the bitch, the minx or just her thousand-year-old self.

Strangely enough—or is it so strange?—there are only a very few American actresses I am truly enthusiastic about. My real favorites are the foreign ones, from Greta Garbo to Sophia Loren, by way of Falconetti, Elissa Landi, Arletty, Edwige Feuillere, Jeanne Moreau, to mention but a few.

Jennifer Jones is, to be sure, 100-percent American. But she has attributes which derive from some far-distant realm, some other-worldly world not unknown to tigers, llamas, unicorns and the like. She leaves an after-image which is unseizable yet durable beyond words. As Kazantzakis said of the geisha—"You look at her and your soul cools off."

Good morning now, Miss Jennifer, and blessings on you! When I arrive in that "world to come where there are guns but no targets," pray God I may see you with even more appreciative eyes than those of a loyal, devoted fan.

RICHARD BURTON
BY SAMMY DAVIS, JR.

RIGHT OFF LET ME SAY loud and clear that he is a friend—a warm, delicate human being who would leap over four mountains to help you along a particular path. I don't want to go into a character analysis of Richard Burton. I don't think I'm close enough to do it. On the other hand, there is not enough to say about him as an actor. In the last few years a notoriety connected with his personal life (which is nobody's business but his own) has contributed to a growing public knowledge of his acting ability, and after years of illuminating every stage he appeared on and brightening some very dim movies the general public has at last discovered with admiration and appreciation the marvelous, great, never-ending well of his talent. This was not always the case.

I first met Richard, casually and fleetingly, at the time of *The Robe*, in which he did a polished professional job, certainly, but there were no great screams in the air and CinemaScope took most of the bows. For me, though, this relatively unknown actor was an experience and I began to "collect" his performances in all the subsequent movies, movies that were for the most part none too good but in which he always stood out like a diamond in the rough. So when I first went to London—I think it was in 1959—it was a pleasant surprise to find I wasn't the only one in the Burton bag. As I sat around late at night until early in the morning with groups of actors—some kings of the English stage, others the princes and pretenders to the throne, still others merely players—the mention of Richard Burton would bring forth stories, recollections, anecdotes, remembrances of past performances, all tinged with the awe and the envy that are the marks of a gigantic talent. In the small, discerning and very demanding circle of his fellow actors, Burton was the best. In the years that followed, that circle has expanded, and the boundless energies of his art have earned him worldwide fame and recognition. Rightly so.

Yes, he is a wonder and a joy to watch. When I went back to see his Hamlet the third or fourth time, I noticed high-school kids sitting in the audience with a copy of the play in their laps in the same way that music students attend concerts and follow the score. During the first scenes, before Hamlet appears, their heads would be bobbing up and down, glancing at the stage, and then at the book, and up to the stage again. And then he made his entrance and the fingers froze on the books, the pages stopped turning, the heads were still, eyes welded to the stage as if each and every spectator had been jolted by a blast of electricity. It was the Burton magic at work again—a zeal for life that comes over on the stage. And I thought then as I think now: There is nothing he can't do.

166

HENRY MILLER
BY NORMAN MAILER

HENRY MILLER was in Edinburgh for the festival in 1962, and, being present myself, I had the chance to see a bit of him for a week and never the good luck to see him again. Therefore, if I write about Miller now, it is not as an expert but an admirer. And in fact I admire not only his work, which I do, enormously (his influence has been profound on a good half of all living American writers), but I admire his personality. He has one of the best personalities I ever met. It is all of a piece, all composed, the way a fine cabinetmaker or a big-game hunter or a tight-rope artist has a personality which is true to itself all the way through. No neurotic push-pull, no maggots in the smile, no envies, no nervousness. It is the kind of composure which suggested he was ready for anything which came on next—did a lion escape from the zoo and walk suddenly into the room, you had the feeling Henry Miller would say, "Say, fellow, you look pretty big coming in here out of the zoo. How's it feel to stretch your legs?"

It is, you see, a personality which is extraordinarily gentle without being the least bit soft, and after a while you get the feeling that Miller always tells the truth, and does it as simply as possible, in a minimum of words, and tempers it only with the desire to be as kind as he can

in the circumstances. In that sense, a poet without talent who has asked him to read his work would probably bother Henry Miller more than the lion, but he would tell the truth, in that slightly rough, slightly humorous voice of his, with the gutty hint of Brooklyn still in the pipes.

So there is Miller, a man of medium size, trim, jaunty in his dress (knickers and a cap in Edinburgh), with a good tough face, big nose, near bald head, looking for all the world like Marx's noble proletarian, like some bricklayer, let us say, you started talking to on a train, and then it turned out he had eighty-two kids and worked at his hobby in spare time—it was translating Sophocles. Then you wonder at the gulf which forever exists between an artist's personality and his work—here particularly the violent, smashing fuck-you gusto of *Tropic of Cancer* and the strong, benign, kindly mood of the man today—and decide that writing is also the purge of what is good and bad in yourself, and the writers who write sweet books, pastorales, idylls, and hymns to the human condition end up snarling old beasts in their senility, whereas Henry, after years of saying out every black thought he had in his head (and some silver ones too), is now forced to defend himself against the allegation that he is angel or saint.

CHARLES LAUGHTON
BY ELSA LANCHESTER

THE PAIN OF TALENT

H E WAS RUGGLES, Henry the Eighth, Bligh, the Hunchback, Javert. Early in his career long ago he was called by a leading English critic "a genius," later by this same critic "a so-called genius," and still later "a self-styled genius." As Charles became a master of his art he learned to abide these slings and arrows of a sometimes outrageous public. He knew it is true that the survival of a style of acting has the shortest life of all the arts and the least use to future generations. Music, painting and literature have roots in the past for the newcomer to turn to, but an actor merely reflects the time he lives in. Charles wished to be more than a mirror of his times—he wished to be more than a medium for the words of others and so he reached out toward painting, toward literature and music. And the pain of his talent was his existing still within the lonely, confining walls of the actor. He reached out for a more complete creativity than the craft of acting allowed, and his pain was the feeling that he would never reach far or high enough.

It is a pain shared by all actors of talent.

MARIAN ANDERSON
BY LEONTYNE PRICE

S O M A N Y T H O U G H T S rush to mind when I think of Marian Anderson. But one in particular is my brightest memory of this magnificent artist and human.

When I was nine years old my mother, who had been reading of the phenomenal success of Marian Anderson, saved for my trip to attend a concert which was to be given in Jackson, Mississippi. Up to then my awareness of concerts was recordings and church musicales. The big day came and, filled with excitement, I was off to Jackson. I had seen pictures of her in the newspapers and heard a record or two, so you can imagine my anticipation of seeing "in person" Marian Anderson.

Needless to say, I was overjoyed, thrilled and inspired. Inspired to want also to attain some measure of success in years to come. Here in this wonderful woman was an inspiration to the many who had wanted a career (and did not believe it possible) and to those who had not thought of it. I was fired with a determination to study my piano lessons more than ever before—and my thoughts of singing reached far beyond the Junior Choir and Glee Club of Oak Park School.

Of course, there are many things which all of us know today about Marian—her tireless tours for many years have opened doors to others, her great debut at the Metropolitan long overdue, her consideration and patience.

Once in a while we meet on tour—London, Washington, D.C., San Francisco, etc.—and it's such a comfortable feeling to be able to talk with her and compare notes.

The deep affection the people of all worlds, all phases of life (musical, political, religious) have for Marian Anderson is legend, and there are no words I can add to enhance that fact.

I never stop recalling that time of preparation which my dear mother made for my trip to Jackson to hear *the* Lovely Lady from Philadelphia.

174

MICHAEL ROMANOFF
BY FRANK SINATRA

Michael Romanoff is an anachronism. In this drip-dry, quickie world, where courtesy and good taste are no longer "in," Michael Romanoff remains one of the last of the true gentlemen. Impeccably tailored (I'd swear he was born in a Homburg), well mannered and gallant, he can make a man feel ten feet tall and a woman feel like a woman.

I met Michael about twenty-two years ago when he was running his old saloon on Rodeo Drive in Beverly Hills. It's funny, but a few minutes after we shook hands I felt as if we had known each other all our lives—it was that kind of chemistry. Since then we have traveled all over the world together, and I have always found him a warm, giving, understanding and comfortable friend. The kind of friend you don't have to talk to if you don't feel like talking, or phone if you don't feel like phoning, but you know he's there and so you're not lonely. Throughout the years, Michael has been a big brother, a stern father, a kind uncle, and, when I'm sick, a Jewish mother.

Through the years there has been a long controversy as to whether Michael Romanoff is the genuine article—a real prince. Well, I don't know a helluva lot about royalty, and I suppose, as the old joke goes, "by princes, he's no prince"—but as a human being, he's more than a prince. He's a King!

176

JULIE ANDREWS
BY ALAN JAY LERNER

L ET ME PUT my cards on the table. An objective appraisal of Julie Andrews will not be found on these premises. For six consecutive years her professional life and mine coexisted on the same stage (the six being two years of *My Fair Lady* in New York, two in London, and two years in *Camelot*). For six consecutive years I was subjected to an unrelenting bombardment of talent, joy and affection which left me with a bad case of jaundiced eyes and as unbiased as an all-white jury in Mississippi.

Julie's theatrical manners, her decorum in rehearsal, are as unique as her talent. She was all of nineteen when *My Fair Lady* went into rehearsal, and she was surrounded by such seasoned virtuosi as Rex Harrison, Stanley Holloway, Cathleen Nesbitt, et al. But however deep her fears, there was not a sign on the surface. Her concentration was never joggled by panic; her general air was always warm and relaxed. If it had not been for the notable absence of profanity by all and sundry (Moss Hart was captain of the alls, and I was captain of the sundries), her professionalism would have totally obscured her youth. Under Moss Hart's sensitive guidance she went a long way during those rehearsals, and her metamorphosis was as great as Eliza's. On opening night in New York she strode upon that stage like a colossus. She was extraordinary, not because she gave such a good performance, but because she gave the best performance she had ever given. In other words, in the parlance of the arena, little Julie turned out to be a "money player." That is to say, a guaranteed riser to the occasion, at her best when it counts most.

As if the subsequent opening in London was not further proof, the premiere of *Camelot* in New York was the clincher. The morning before the first New York performance, Fritz and I delivered to her a brand-new song! A few minutes later she was on the phone. I started to count down to zero and prepare for the explosion. None was forthcoming. She apologized for calling so early, but told me she simply had to let me know how much she loved the song. Not a word did she mention about the problems of memorizing it and digesting it in time for the performance the next night. It was a dazzling display even for Julie, who memorizes faster than anything with wheels and springs, and projects it with a clarity of diction that is every lyric writer's dream.

When she came to Hollywood and won the Academy Award for her first picture, it must have been dreadfully discouraging for some of her fellow Thespians to see an actress achieve stardom with nothing to offer but pure talent, real industry and an uncorrupted heart—let alone being

further handicapped by a weakness for proper speech. And it must have been infuriating to the press agents and image-makers to discover that the incredible sweetness and dignity that shine through her performing talents are, offscreen, genuine incredible sweetness and dignity. How jarring to find the image she projects is actually the person she is!

At this writing Julie is not only a star but the number-one star in the world. It so happens that the theatre is a profession where we drink to success, but the chaser is envy; and to become the number-one star is really asking for it. But Julie is different. For some lovely reason everyone, theatrical or civilian, is genuinely happy for her.

My own feeling is that any world that gives her its heart has its heart in the right place. And that's a very nice thing to know. After all, if what the world really wants is Julie, then Julie is a cause for optimism.

JONATHAN WINTERS
BY MICKEY ROONEY

Expression, warmth, humility, creativeness and genius is Jonathan Winters. Too many people, things, places, dreams, visions, all of life itself, fall into either orderly or disorderly patterns. However, there are exceptions to all rules, for when an individual becomes truly individual, dreams can become things, visions can become places, and all of life rises to the crescendo of the mind put to the palette, where the brush of the extemporaneous can unfearfully apply the strokes of giving of himself.

TUESDAY WELD
BY TUESDAY WELD

I N HER KNOWN RIGHT

1.   How would I know?

2.   Carried on a lot.

3.   Socks and shoes.

4.   Work's a bore.

5.   But I'm adored.

6.   I can't read.

7.   Still can't or even smile.

8.   I think I should go away for a while.

9.   I retired, quit, for once and for all.

10.   I'd had my share.

11.   When quitting's fair.

12.   Tore my mother's hair.

13.   Well, I didn't really care.

14.   Grown and free, hated everybody.

15.   I saw a tree.

16.   Tried to kill my mother.

17.   Fell in love for once and all.

18.   Thought I'd leave him for another.

19.   I did.

20.   Had a birthday.

21.   Now I know real love for once and all.

21½. I painted the tree of memory, and gave as life a gift, it away.

22.   I saw another tree.

BERT LAHR
BY PADDY CHAYEFSKY

THEY ARE APT to call Lahr a great clown, meant as a compliment, I'm sure, but it's not my idea of one. I never saw a clown I thought funny, or even sad. I don't like tramp acts; I find wistfulness tiresome on the stage. I know that when they call Lahr a clown they're implying he's something more than a mere comedian, that through his actor's art he somehow reveals the elemental poignancy of the human condition. Well, I don't think the human condition is elementally poignant any more than I think it is wistful. I find the whole clown thing sentimental and something of a put-down when applied to Lahr. He's far more than a great clown; he's a great comic. Technically, he's a musical-comedy comedian, a sketch comic, and consequently cannot be identified with any one characterization, or even any one costume, as, for example, is the case with Chaplin. In any one night's performance, Lahr barrels onto the stage a low comedian in one scene, minces off a mime in the next, a zany comic in the next, and an expert legitimate actor in the sketch after that. He has the whole bag of tricks, the burlesque takes and slow burns, the low-comedy bits and *stücks* expected of any sketch comic. He has the rubber face for mugging, a bellowing baritone that can be heard in the theatre across the street, and he can leer at a towering showgirl with the best of them. But the thing that distinguishes Lahr is not the lowness of his comedy or his medieval mastery of it; the thing about Lahr is his curious delicacy. He walks a very fine line indeed in his performing. Like W. C. Fields, he scorns any sentimental cushion for his comedy. I've never known Lahr to play for anything so blunt as pathos. He's never the fool or the poor put-upon fellow. If anything, his characterizations are relentlessly unsympathetic. He plays coarse or cunning or greedy, the lecher rather than the innocent (a far more precise depiction of the human condition than that of the poignant clown). One slip, and the whole sketch becomes shabby, even ugly. Well, I've never seen Lahr miss his footing yet. Lahr's not a clown at all; he's a performer, an *artiste*, a remarkable actor and, to my mind, the funniest man on the American stage.

PAUL NEWMAN
BY STEWART STERN

MOST PEOPLE SUFFER from an excess of never being looked at."

This face never looks at itself in the mirror to admire its lagoon-blue eyes. It is shaved blindly each morning in the shower by an unsoaped razor, its owner's sense of touch, and the watchfulness of God.

It is to be found on the front of the head of a tactful, tolerant, complex, loving man who goes at his days as if they were lions and he had to slay seven by nightfall.

What follows is an unpremeditated, unfinished sketch of himself put together from snippets of letters he wrote in the early days of his career when everything was for the first time.

DATELINE: *"Progress-on-the-Backslide"*

"I'm glad you liked the show because I'm going to give up acting."

DATELINE: *"Nasser-on-the-Suez"*

"Booze is terribly expensive.
Twin beds.
Joanne's hair dye has yet to arrive and she's black at the roots, which is wonderful for her black disposition.
Twin beds.

Never think for a minute that it's fun to be successful, old chap.
'Heavy falls the head that wears the crown' uh 'heavy *lies* the head that wears the crown' uh
'heavy is the head' uh 'heavy *lays* the head that wears the crown.'
Twin beds."

(The above was about hotel accommodations on location.)

"They stand in front of the hotel all day, staring in at the lobby or hollering upstairs into unknown windows, eyeballs, hundreds of them, peering through the fence. Most people suffer from an excess of never being looked at and here we suffer the opposite extreme. As always, we want the notoriety on our own terms. 'Please notice the delicacy of the features, the size of the talent, but then do not linger, and heaven forbid you touch the merchandise!' "

"Joanne just appeared in some kind of mask designed to draw all of the moisture out of her face. She wanted me to lick an envelope because she couldn't open her mouth far enough to get her tongue out."

DATELINE: *"Lying-on-the-Couch"*

"I am beginning to get sick of acting, not because it's a fraud, but because I am no longer able to find anything that I haven't done before—I have *had* me on the screen in all my facets, and there's nothing unexposed of me. All I can do now is dig into the make-up kit and put on a false nose or add a regional dialect. Some actors of our generation, Guinness maybe, or Olivier, never seem to exhaust themselves. Their inventions are always original."

"The fun boy himself is presently having more fun than all the poor people in the world together. Because, boy, once you force yourself to have fun—*you have it!* You learn it like anything else—playing marbles, for instance, or swallowing swords, or putting out cigarettes on your tongue, all those fun things. A barrel full of laughs. Keep laughing, Charlie, because tomorrow you might be calmly examining your insides from the outside. And that is our lil thought for today."

(The above written during the acceleration of nuclear testing.)

"Joanne's mummy just left after three weeks with us. They have a lovely word for 'mother-in-law' here—*ma belle mère*—beautiful mother."

"Whatever is going to become of us all, I wonder? You and I will sit on our respective tombstones, I guess, and at that time I *might* be able to tell you about me."

Postcard from a ship at sea:

"We are drin

      king

         quite

            a

              b

                i

                  t."

LILLIAN HELLMAN
BY WILLIAM STYRON

DEFINITION AND A FRAGMENT OF DIALOGUE

T RADE LAST, *usually abbr. t.l., a verbal game played by prenubile young girls in certain schools of the United States, which involves an elaborate by-play having to do with the exchange and withholding of compliments. There are usually two active participants. Let us assume that Alice has heard Bessie say a very nice thing about Clara. Upon next encountering Clara, Alice will say in a tantalizing tone: "Clara dear, I have a t.l. for you." Clara at this point will be anxious to know both the nature of the compliment and especially its donor (Bessie), who ideally is a girl whom one distantly admires. The rules of the game, however, prevent Alice from divulging anything of the secret until Clara has responded by telling Alice of a compliment she has heard about her. This must be a real compliment from someone else, not an item of praise fabricated on the spur of the moment and falsely attributed to another. Thus, if what Bessie had said to Alice was, "I think Clara is such a peach of a girl, so thoughtful and kind!" this*

192

sentiment will not be made known to Clara unless first she repeats what she has actually been told about Alice, viz: "Dorothy said she thinks you're just a whiz at seaming bloomers, Alice!" Alice thereupon trades her compliment last, hence the name of the game.

—WEBBER AND BRUSEY'S
Complete Cyclopedia of Folk Games
(1923, rev. ed. 1947)

WILLIAM STYRON *(on the telephone)*: Lil?

LILLIAN HELLMAN *(in a voice with a fine reckless exuberance, like a hug)*: Hi, dear, how are you? I have a t.l. for you already!

W.S.: Wonderful! What is it?

L.H.: What do you *mean*, what is it? You're supposed to give me *my* t.l. first! My God! You'd think I never taught you this game!

W.S.: Suppose I don't have any t.l.'s?

L.H.: Oh come on, cut the crap! You told me last week you had bushels of t.l.'s! What's the matter with you anyway! *(The tone is jocular but there is a faint edge of annoyance in the voice, very faint.)*

W.S.: All right, well, yes. Um. Well, yes, I do have one really. Really, a very wonderful t.l., I think, Lil.

L.H.: Come on, *give* it to me. *(Real impatience.)*

W.S.: I think you're going to love it.

L.H.: *Ach,* you tease! You kill me! Another one from that doorman who said my dog was well behaved. Another one from Herbert Hoover's great-grandson. *Oy gevalt!*

W.S.: No, this one's from—

L.H.: *(vaguely touched with despondency)*: I'm a very sick woman. Now this morning I get this—

194

W.S.: It's from Henry Singleton.

L.H.: (*after a long pause*): Well . . . yes. He's . . . a very attractive man. A fine lawyer too. And quite bright. (*Another pause, rather somber.*) What did he say?

W.S.: He said he knew of no woman alive who had so many admirers and who had such radiance and warmth and generosity of spirit. I might put that in Roddy's book.

L.H.: Oh that's nice. That's very nice! What he said, that is.

W.S.: The thing is, Lil, it's true, it really is. No one, no woman I know of, is the recipient of so much honest affection and love. If we except only Jacqueline Kennedy, Elizabeth Taylor, Margaret Mead and Madam Pandit.

L.H.: Now don't be facetious. Henry Singleton always was a flatterer. But . . . Well, that is awfully nice.

W.S.: The point is, neither of us is being facetious. I mean it's a simple fact. You have almost more admirers than any woman anyone knows. So *Time* magazine hates you, who could care less? Doesn't all this make the morning a little less—

L.H.: Yes, it does! Now I have a t.l. for you.

W.S.: (*eagerly*): Who's it from?

L.H.: Just a minute, dear, there's the other telephone.

W.S.: (*anxiously now*): Who's it from?

L.H.: Look, I'll call you right back, O.K.? It's Sam again.

W.S.: (*in a resigned voice*): Another one of your admirers. (*He slowly hangs up and broods aloud*): I suppose that for that book I could write a lot of ornate stuff about Lillian's iron-bound honesty and the great dignity of her bearing and her awesome sense of justice—all of which would be true. I think, however, I will simply begin by saying that she is one of the few people left who, in the midst of the general madness, retain that mysterious yet obdurate sense of *play* which creates for herself and for others the saving grace of joy.

LEONARD BERNSTEIN
BY RICHARD AVEDON

THAT A MAN OF Leonard Bernstein's quality is so often called "Lenny" by his detractors indicates that he has not been cautious, that he has been trusting, accessible, remained vulnerable, and left available in and to himself what lesser men, out of fear, close off. Alienation being the easy way out, he has taken the hard way, and it has left him free to compose, conduct, instruct, build, and above all remain connected to the needs of his time. He has worked close to them, using himself completely, and with a consistent sense of responsibility and selflessness that amounts to courage.

Okay.

We once shared a box at the Metropolitan for the opera season—a pretty funny box, since my wife and I know as much about music as the Bernsteins know about photography. He decided, one rainy Vineyard morning, to our joy, to give us a pre-season lesson we wouldn't forget. He played, sang and acted every role in *Tosca*. It took three hours, and ended with his leaping a full foot from the coffee table to the floor (the parapets of Sant'Angelo) and breaking his ankle. Well, we never forgot.

He is a man who has never stopped giving—that is to say, strengthening whomever he reaches. Because of his discipline and genius, and the fact that they happened in the twentieth century, he has brought more people to the power of music (it sounds extravagant to say this, but I know it is true) than any other man in the history of the world.

196

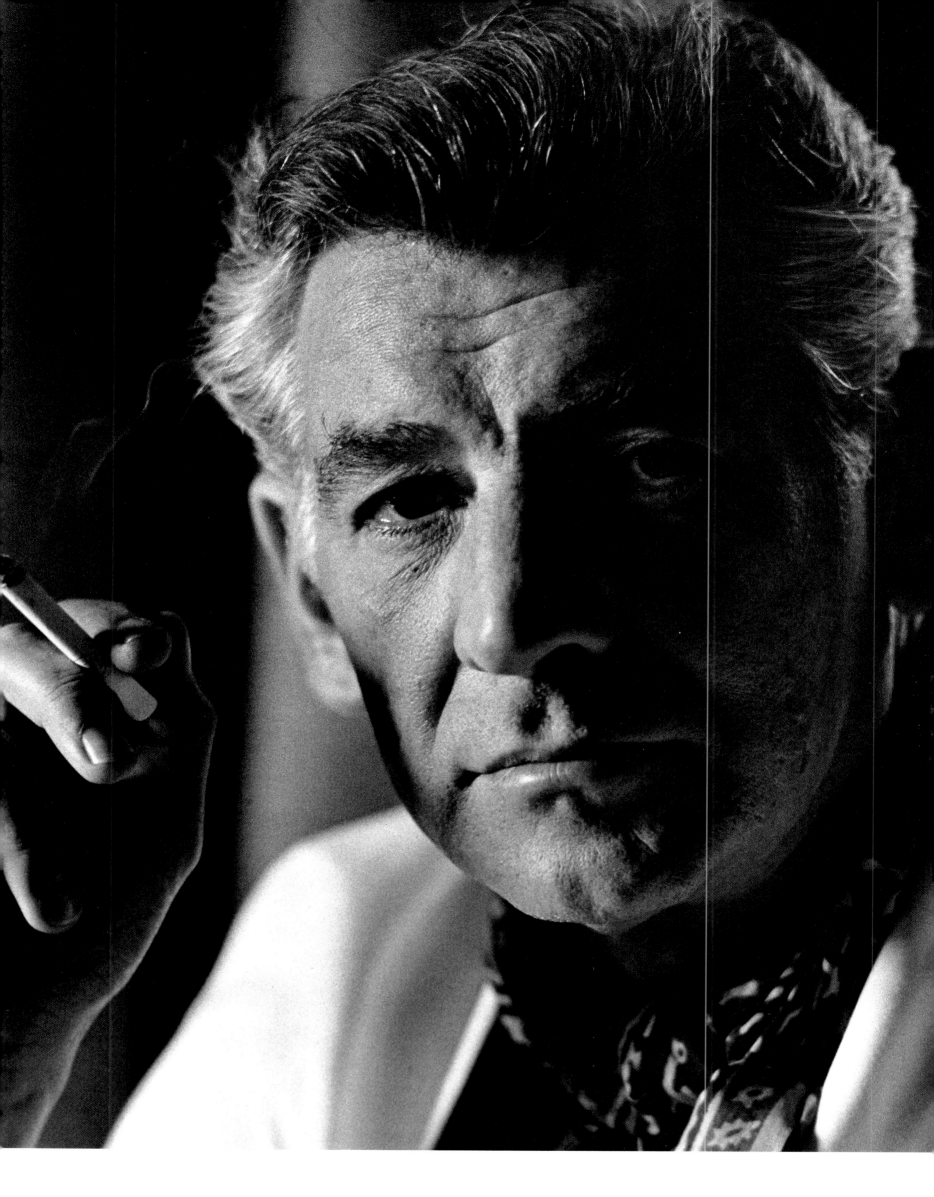

JOSEPH L. MANKIEWICZ
BY NUNNALLY JOHNSON

THERE WERE ONCE three Mankiewiczes at Paramount. But Erna defected to marriage, and Herman, after an occasionally brilliant, always lively career, passed on. One of Herman's few gentle emotions was his pride in the accomplishments of his younger brother Joe.

He had reason for this pride. Joe was one of the first of the screenwriters of consequence to take on the responsibilities of directing too. (If the records contain an instance in which a first-rate director became also a first-rate writer it must be in very fine print.) The measure of Joe's success in this double responsibility was in his winning of Oscars for both writing and directing in successive years, for two memorable pictures, *A Letter to Three Wives* and *All About Eve*.

In time he took on still a third accountability: he became the producer of his pictures. As a generality, no greater mistake is possible for a film-maker already in charge of two-thirds of the troika: in the event of a Disappointment, it is next to impossible to convince everyone that the failure of the project may be traced to the incompetence of the hairdresser. It is a mistake that he is not likely to make again.

But whether WOW IN DENVER OR NSG IN CHI, Joe's pictures all have the flavor of quality, the quality of a superior and professional intelligence. Even his few Disappointments have been disappointments on a respectable level, for his aims, once he was in position to exercise them without restrictions, have been high and his achievements impressive. Today, a Mankiewicz picture is one to command the most serious attention possible in film-making.

JUDY GARLAND
BY EDWARD ALBEE

ONCE UPON A TIME—1950, I think—I was sitting in the balcony of what was probably the Capitol Theatre, in New York, watching a Judy Garland movie which my memory tells me was *Summer Stock*. In the course of that film I witnessed an intensity of communication between artist and audience that is single in my memory.

I can't remember, now, whether the song was "Lonely Star" or "Get Happy," but it doesn't matter. What does matter is that when Garland finished singing, the audience watching that film was breathless for a moment and then, to a person, burst into sustained applause.

My reaction to Garland's art has varied over the years; it has risen as high as unqualified adulation and sunk as low as intense pleasure; but, for all of it—including a superb August night at the Palladium in 1960—nothing has instructed and gratified me more than the time she convinced a bunch of afternoon movie-watchers that a strip of celluloid was the real thing.

200

GEORGE ABBOTT
BY HAROLD PRINCE

Acc
According to George Abbott's autobiography
—*Mister Abbott*—he was born in Forestville, New York,
not far from Rochester, on June 25, 1887.

Now a dominant quality in that autobiography and in
interviews with George Abbott over the years has been
terseness, an almost exasperating predilection for forth-
rightness, so I don't intend to question that fact.
However—and since I came to work for him as a not so
glorified office boy in 1948, eighteen years ago, and since he gave me my first job as a second
assistant stage manager, periodic boosts up to first assistant stage manager, and since ultimately
my partner, Bobby Griffith, and I shared office space with George (correction: Mr. Abbott it
was then) from 1954 on, when we were producing *The Pajama Game* out of his office and

paying him neither rent nor even telephone bills—I consider myself a self-appointed historian, and there are facts that I possess that did not find their way into his book except by deduction.

The first fact is that George Abbott has a greater record of success and a longer record of activity than any other producer, director or playwright in the theatre today anywhere in this world. How has he done it? He's done it by being terse and uncomplicated, by taking the "easiest way" out—by working hard and often for himself without regard for "the competition." What other people are doing is interesting to him only if it works and it's new. I've heard him recently responding acutely to something new, or something old, which still works on the stage and which he didn't think could anymore, with curiosity and enthusiasm.

George is not interested in what show is in trouble out of town, or whether there are too many hits when he's getting ready to open a new play, or whether this playwright has lost his touch or that director's in a slump. He is not petty. He is not a gossip.

It used to astonish me, when we talked about the plays we'd done together, that he would never measure one against the other—this one was better than that in this respect. He is vaguely interested in why the failures failed, not in the least interested in why the successes succeeded, but not really interested, once a play has opened, in any of the whys or wherefores. One of his plays won the Pulitzer Prize for him. He did not set out to win the Pulitzer Prize with the next play, to compete with that accolade, to exceed himself.

Rather, he did as he has done over all the years: he forgot that award, that play, and went back to work.

He is no snob. A drama is not better than a musical comedy, a musical comedy no better than a lightweight farce. Each has its place; each must work within its own demands and no more.

GEORGE ABBOTT
BY HAROLD PRINCE

He is considered by many unapproachable. This astonishes him. He isn't unapproachable, and many, many people know that. Perhaps his looks (poor fellow) militate against just anyone slapping him on the back and saying, "Hiya, George." Perhaps his terseness. But let me tell you, they are reassuring: it's awfully nice to have him around.

The most irrelevant fact is the fact of his birth date. The real fact is that he is young, that he has chosen for good sensible reasons to work with young people, composers and lyricists, new undiscovered actors, set and costume designers, conductors and orchestrators. He has advised them, edited them, rewritten them, calmed them down, taught them the foolishness of panic, encouraged them—*bet on them*—and, in return, he has moved along with them creatively from one period to another. He doesn't consciously think what is the newest trend in the theatre and how do I emulate it. He thinks instead of the energy and the joy of theatre work that's likely to come from young, ambitious, untested people, and he takes his chances with them.

Perhaps that is it; perhaps that would have saved me all these words. George Abbott takes his chances in the theatre. He always has. The list of people who started with him is greater, I am certain, than the list of people who started with all the other producers, directors and authors in the theatre of our time.

For less relevant facts, I refer you to Who's Who in America.

LENA HORNE
BY JOAN SUTHERLAND

I HAVE SEEN Lena Horne perform many times. As an artist I admire and respect her enormously. I have met Lena, alas, only a few times (which I hope will be remedied) and as a woman I took to her immediately. She is a great singer of songs, one of the greatest of our time. Her musicianship, her innate rhythm, her great sense of style—all are impeccable. She is a great beauty. Her figure is, without exaggeration, divine, and she has immense chic. She is a wonderful wife and mother. All these qualities added together amount to a very remarkable woman indeed.

Although I perform in an entirely different musical sphere, I ought to be the perfect choice to pay tribute to Lena Horne because, apart from the fact that no one can admire her more than I, we have a great thing in common—the loving help given to us over the years by our husbands. But I am not a writer and therefore, I am sad to say, I cannot do her the justice I would like and which is her due. I hope, however, that she will gather from this how deeply I admire the perfection of her talent, her great warmth as an artist and how much I feel I owe her for all the pleasure she has given me.

206

GEORGE STEVENS
BY IVAN MOFFAT

When I accused him of pretentious modesty he was delighted and adopted the phrase for use against himself. (I told an actor this. "George the Obscure?" he suggested. Perfect.)

George indeed has something of the hidden monument—a vaulted hiding place of strengths and secrets disguised within a casual, lumbering sort of golf-course bonhomie (his ball is in a sand bunker, but you have the feeling he has placed it there). Not because he is contrariwise and devious (he is, and one-eighth Comanche) but because facility and ease are strangers to his awkward genius; his exploration lies in the area of our inarticulate striving. (He is a gadget-lover rejected by gadgets.) There, in the famous and deceptively leisurely style peculiar to himself, comedy and light tragedy become compassionately intertwined.

His laughter comes from a sense of the absurd in man's obedience to his own rules and from an antic awareness of the incongruous in George himself. (Location hunting in the Sierras: "Who would think, looking at this five-Cadillac caravan of businessmen, that I was trying to find a good lake to drown a pregnant girl in?")

He goes to the ball game, drives a Porsche slowly, says "Howdy, partner" and means it, owns property in the Valley and grows alfalfa somewhere.

And there are periods when this clumsy, sensitive, kind-seeming man becomes a figure with an eye of liquid rage, a face red with anger and with the deeper embarrassment of its anger, slow to subside and—even in stress—not always comprehensible or fair. Strange.

And when, after many months, he has finished what is lightly called directing his film, he starts to make it: imprisons himself in cutting rooms, in the dark of projection rooms, day and night, sometimes for a year, ceaselessly reweaving; that's when the infinity of his capacity is best seen and least observed. At ten or eleven at night he will come out of the studio and, like as not, dine alone.

He forgets no one, although his microscopic memory is abetted, one feels, by suspicion (his earliest recall is of the San Francisco earthquake of 1906).

He is not much seen in Hollywood—and by choice, socially, hardly ever.

One thing you can say: People who have spent a little time with him are more inclined to think they know him than those who have spent much.

George is famous, but he is not well known.

LEE REMICK
BY HORTON FOOTE

L<small>EE REMICK</small> has the ability to make very moving a certain kind of American woman, sometimes seen in the cities, but usually found on farms, in small cities or towns, an American beauty, unaware of her beauty, without narcissism, unafraid of hard work, of poverty, or of being exposed to heat or cold, the wind or the sun. When you see her in such a part you are reminded of women you have seen in certain sections of America where women have to work like men in the fields, in the factories, or in the homes, and yet manage to retain their femininity. She brings the same dignity of spirit and lack of sentimentality to these women that you find when Willa Cather and William Faulkner write of them in their novels, or in the poems and prose of William Carlos Williams and e.e. cummings. It is unimportant, of course, but curious that nothing in her personal background would seem to make her knowledgeable or sympathetic with such people or their circumstances, but know them she does and she makes you know them, understand and value them.

DANNY KAYE
BY SYLVIA FINE KAYE

ALL MY HUSBANDS

BY SYLVIA FINE KAYE, MRS. DANNY

How could I dream, that faraway day
When I married the unknown Danny Kaye,
That I was casting *my* lot
With that of a commercial pilot?
The only entertainer with a choice today
of NBC, CBS, or TWA
. . . or the Boston Symphony—
Which he conducts offhand with a command that is chronic,
Ditto the New York—or any old Philharmonic
Tho' he can't read a note
Which puts him in the boat
Of conducting by ear—which, when all is said and gone,
Is clearly more difficult than using a baton.

But should he fall off a clef
Or turn tone deaf
He could always get a job as Number One Chef
In a Chinese restaurant . . .
But—

The Transcendental Oriental
Le Vrai Chinois
Where they eschew Chop Suey and chop Chun Fah,
He cooks a twenty-course dinner
Which he says makes you thinner
With the spiel of a real Billy Graham
Of exotica delicious
With names so suspicious
I'd much rather eat 'em than say 'em.

So my husband the pilot, conductor and sprite
Comes home from rehearsal and cooks every night
. . . Unless he's wanted in surgery . . .

Where, officially asked
Gowned and masked
He'll study a pancre-a-techtomy—
Well, I dig saving stamps
But the mem'ry of clamps
Seems a very odd thing to collect ta me!

But I love his collection of children's affection
Givèn from the teen-age to wean-age to diaper
In all the world's places, their hearts in their faces
for UNICEF'S peripatetic Pied Piper.

DANNY KAYE
BY SYLVIA FINE KAYE

So what was he doing, my dear Mr. Moto
When Roddy McDowall was flexed for this photo?
Was he . . .
Learning a Largo for Symphony Corchestra?
Decoding the argot of a flight weather forechestra?
List'ning to children sing songs that he taught 'em?
Joining the Dodgers for post-game Post Maughtem?
Conferring with Dr. C. Mayo at Clinic?
Or caught between cookstove and icebox and sinick?

Don't bet any money—just take a quick glance, sir
On page 254, you'll find the full answer!

But whatever he does it's relaxed and resilient
Charming, disarming, beguiling or brilliant
A singer who dances, a dancer who sings
An actor at ease with impossible things
Quick-tempered, quixotic, delightful despotic
Ascetic, kinetic, chaotic.

Who's Who which lets nobody seedy in
Lists him as "actor, comedian"
But as wife and as writer, as critic and fan
I'd list him as *Danny Kaye—Renaissance Man.*

MARLON BRANDO
BY JAMES BALDWIN

I FIRST MET Marlon Brando in the spring of 1944, when, for reasons having to do with youth and confusion, I spent a lot of time hanging around Manhattan's New School for Social Research. Marlon was a member of the Dramatic Workshop of the New School and was then studying with Erwin Piscator. It was not long before we struck up a kind of laconic friendship—we were both very shy—and somewhat distrustfully informed each other of the shape of our futures: he was to become a great actor, I was to become a great writer. (Young people use words like that.) I don't doubt that the likelihood of his ever becoming an actor seemed faint to me. Marlon impressed me as being a very nice, rather odd-looking boy, with a very odd name, from out West somewhere, and I thought that he was probably, without being willing to admit it, a poet. I thought of all actors as being embarrasingly extroverted; this was emphatically not the case with Marlon. Time passed, we kept up a sporadic connection with each other, and I finally saw Marlon for the first time on the professional stage in Maxwell Anderson's *Truckline Café.* The play was pretty bad, but Marlon's performance was a great revelation to me and gave me my first real intimation of what acting was all about. He played a kind of shriveled, psychoneurotic war veteran who eventually murders his faithless wife. He was so shriveled, so lame and so stricken that, after the curtain, I was vastly relieved and somewhat surprised to find him backstage looking perfectly able and healthy and with that crooked grin on his face.

But it is irrelevant for me to discuss Marlon as an actor; and I find that it is quite beyond me to discuss him as a friend. What goes into the making of a friendship is very deep and quiet and it really cannot be talked about. In fact, I don't think that it *should* be talked about. Which reduces me to saying that I love and admire Marlon very much, partly, no doubt, because of the impressive tenacity with which he tries honorably to deal with the conundrum of his life, but principally, finally, I suppose, simply because he is Marlon, and there's only one of him, for only one time. For me, he's a beautiful cat and I guess, finally, that that's all one friend can say about a friend.

216

NATALIE WOOD
BY ARNOLD SCHULMAN

S HE SINGS the worst close-harmony "Down by the Old Mill Stream" of anybody I ever heard. She doesn't know how to heat up a take-out order from a Chinese restaurant. She has a wide variety of shaggy dogs and friends. Some love her. Some use her.

She is the stubborn, fragile blade of grass we have all seen piercing through the middle of the sidewalk, a feat made even more remarkable when one considers that not only is the sidewalk a path for travelers, going from everyplace to anywhere, but it is also the place where bums relieve themselves, men in dinner jackets spit when nobody is looking, four-inch heels grind chewing gum, soot and the evidence of uncurbed dogs into the pores of the cement. A place to play in safety or a child's garden of neurosis?

And yet somehow this indomitable, adorable woman-child, product of a system, has managed to come through.

How? Why?

In search of the sun? In awe of the moon.

JASON ROBARDS
BY BUDD SCHULBERG

I CAN IMAGINE Richard Burton as a director, following in the footsteps of Olivier and Gielgud. I can see Christopher Plummer directing, and perhaps Marlon Brando directing again. But I can never think of Jason Robards as anything but *actor*. There are some people who seem born to a single calling, as John Paul Jones was born to fight sailing ships and Valery Brumel was born to soar like a human feather over the high-jump bar. What they do is what they are. Even in a private talk or with a photograph, you look at Jason and Jason looks back at you and he is *acting*. I don't mean acting in contrast to being himself. I find the actor so ingrained in Jason that when he is acting, on or off the stage, he is being himself.

Jason Robards isn't a thinker. He isn't a writer. He isn't a Studio methodist. He isn't chic. It isn't a pose for him to wear an old baseball cap to a ball game, or to pick out a tune from the Twenties on his uke at parties. He's that godsend to writers—unabashed nonintellectual raw material who begs you the writer to form him to your design.

In an age when too many actors think too much, self-pity themselves too much, indulge their neuroses—somewhere I think Burton called it "gnawing at their own bellies"—Jason is a passionate professional who doesn't forget there is an audience out there. A refreshing antidote to the underacting pause-and-mumble school, Jason Robards is, to stretch a word, *outuitive*.

No one would ever confuse him with a British stylist, a French *emoteur* or a Stanislavski preparer. A good look at Jason shows you an American phenom. He's so American it's only the flint and the glint in him that keeps him from being *American*. He's as star-spangled as Willie Mays and the Oak Park Hemingway, as sour-mash whiskey and Brownie McGhee singing "Just a Closer Walk with Thee," as the old mongoose Archie Moore and the riotous prince of stage and screen Jack Barrymore. He doesn't command the grand manner of Barrymore or the shifty grace of the true fighter-performer Archie Moore, but when you think of American actors on the scene now that the Bogies and the Garfields are gone, you've got to be encouraged that Jason is around. Jason the music man, Jason the iceman cometh, Jason the inelegant Casanova, Jason the banjo-strumming clown, Jason the disenchanted, Jason the happy boozer living it up with Plummer and O'Toole, Jason the dedicated pro unafraid to play big (we're talking acting now) in a world of tiny alices.

I remember the first impact of Jason Robards in the Quintero—off-Broadway *Iceman*. It seemed to me then that Jason was made for O'Neill. O'Neill is the most baffling writer in the American theatre. He is the Dreiser of our dramatists. He is clumsy and repetitious, and his conception of the Americanization of Greek tragedy is often primitive and heavy-handed. But his boozy optimists are authentic Americans in search of a sale, for whom the no-sale sign must inevitably ring up as the curtain falls. He was forever writing the death of a salesman. Jason attacks this theme with verve and gusto. Eugene O'Neill can't think too much and neither can Jason, but the chemistry of writing and playing creates a sense of profundity. Jason plays the fun as well as the doom, and his unquestioning acceptance of the playwright makes difficult lines easy and long speeches hang together with vitality.

But it was Jason's work in O'Neill's *Long Day's Journey into Night* that convinced me that he could play Manley Halliday in *The Disenchanted*. Our months together preparing the play for Broadway were rather unusual for author-star relationships: we got along supremely well. There were no frills or hidden sides to Jason. He was frank about his shortcomings. He did not have the elegance, the Prince-of-Wales style, the sophisticated charm associated with a "Manley Halliday" at the height of his literary fame in the golden Twenties. He had no real affinity with writers or their second cousins, the intellectuals. Jason's idols were Barrymore and Freddie

March. He admitted that he could not relate to *littérateurs*; instead he would "use" the image of the fallen Barrymore, or of his own father, the irrepressible ex-stage-and-screen star Jason Robards, Sr. (who played Jason's solicitous editor in our production). I admired the way Jason battled his way through *The Disenchanted*. Maybe he wasn't quite as insouciant and stylish as his critics may have wished. But hundreds of times before demanding audiences I heard Jason deliver his climactic, final speech, where had to balance delicacy with tragedy, and each time I marveled at the way he moved them and held them in pin-drop silence.

Whenever I watched Jason "wrapping them up" in that crucial monologue building to the final curtain, I thought of an early hotel-bedroom conference on the road. I had launched into a rather involved literary-psychological explanation of Manley Halliday's motivation. Suddenly Jason stopped me. "Wait a minute, Budd, you're forgetting something." He tapped his temple not disdainfully but matter-of-factly. "I've got nothing up here." Then he pointed to his belly: "Give it to me *here*." In an age of overcerebration and self-indulgence, this was a healthy confession. Jason isn't an actor's actor, or a director's actor, or a Studio actor; he's a visceral actor —what he would call a gut actor. In the boxing lingo Jason digs; he is like one of those rare club fighters with so much heart and so much drive and so much punch that he fights his way into the inner circle, like Carmen Basilio, bloody and unbowed after fifteen rounds of danger and glory.

"You write the lines, you make up in your head what is supposed to be in my head," he said to me. "All I can do is indicate what you're after." Then characteristically he turned it into a raucous joke. "Remember me—the last of the great indicators." And Jason Robards, the compelling tragedian with a yen to be a song-and-dance man, would do a little shuffle-off-to-Buffalo.

These are the many faces of Jason Robards I see in Roddy McDowall's reflective portrait.

ALFRED DRAKE
BY FREDERIC MORTON

A DAZZLEMENT OF contradictions sits on the opposite page: one of the greatest stage musicians who is an aficionado of the word; the sovereign—too often the absentee lord—of musical comedy, with the brain and the semantic lust of the Shakespearean scholar; the leap and thrust of a boy athlete who broods encyclopedically; a d'Artagnan magnificent with flourishes, his beard like a plume—and a mind modern and labyrinthine with Freud and Pirandello; a Renaissance man who can't drive a car (though what Renaissance man could?); a Latin in ancestry and *esprit*, yet with the blue-eyed gaze of an Anglican philosopher; a dynamo of health and, alack, of insomnia; the master of Broadway at its most American, questing for classic Italy. In brief, a Kismet-haunted Hamlet, kissing Kate in Oklahoma.

TAMMY GRIMES
BY JULIUS MONK

T AMMY GRIMES is a star, they say, and a star, according to Mr. Webster, is "a heavenly body seen as a small fixed point of light . . . especially one that is distantly seen." Heavenly body? Who can argue. Small? Yes! Fixed point of light? If Tammy is ever that, so is Tinkerbell. One that is distantly seen? No, her orbit is drawing closer, the star is rising, the luminescence glowing brighter. Perhaps more a comet, though something fiery in her being makes me think so, appearing once in a lifetime. Of the hundreds of actors and actresses who have auditioned for me in the past thirty addled years, I might be inclined to say Tammy Grimes was/is the one whose singularity indicated not a meteoric rise and shining but the substantial stellar stuff to conquer (and place in her personal firmament) the legitimate and musical theatre, television, radio, records, and cabaret. To transpose a popular lyrical echo of the Thirties:

> "She's much too much—
> And oh so very, very—
> To ever find—
> In Webster's Dic-tion-ary!"

227

DONALD PLEASENCE
BY HAROLD PINTER

PLEASENCE MOVES from stillness, from loss, from blankness, to savagery and obsession with a speed which is astonishing and which fully justifies itself. He doesn't have to worry about surveying a bridge before he can cross it. He moves and is over. That's it. And we go with him.

But the fits of ferocity and obsessional concentration are never merely fireworks. They come out of the gentleness, the delicacy, the quietude, the surprise within him as an actor.

I've not only watched his complete under-the-skinness from the front, but I've acted with him. He listens, he watches, he's unavoidable. He has two things absolutely—most rare—belief and courage. He'll go for it and do it. He is it and remains it. And he's a quite brilliant comedian.

228

DAVID O. SELZNICK
BY S. N. BEHRMAN

THE LATE Bernard Berenson divided the human race—"bipeds," he called them—into two categories: "life-diminishing" and "life-enhancing." David Oliver Selznick belonged overwhelmingly to the latter. Someone who did not know him asked me to describe him and all I could think of to say was: "He was larger than life." So he was and he abetted it. It was an unthinking, involuntary essence possessed by genius. Among the multitude of gifted men I worked with in Hollywood during its great years, he loomed up: gargantuan in size, in vitality, in humor and meticulous in craftsmanship. I worked with him on *A Tale of Two Cities*. He seemed to know the book by heart: he was always coming up with some phrase, some nuance which I and the others involved had overlooked or forgotten.

Whatever subject you happened upon in conversation with David, he rode it like a surfboard and everything was irradiated with humor. In Hollywood in those days I was a *New York Times* addict. Whenever David came into my office, he'd find me reading the *Times*. One morning he said, "When you die, Sam, *The New York Times* will be shredded and cast over your grave instead of flowers." After *Gone With the Wind* was produced, I was having a drink with him one day and I said, "The money must be coming in on that pretty fast." David said, "You know, the other day when I gave Jock Whitney a check for the first million dollars of profits, he was as delighted as if he'd never seen a million dollars before!"

I have been living on this anecdote for years. It is unfailing. So was David O. Selznick.

230

MABEL MERCER
BY WARREN BEATTY

Although she has been my kept woman for some time (at the moment I keep her in a room called the Upstairs at the Downstairs on 56th Street), I lacked what was necessary to introduce myself to her until a couple of years ago. When you hear her sing, you know, she becomes also your daughter, mother, wife and accountant.

The first time I saw her was at one of those nightclub openings when a loud singer coerced her into singing unprepared. The pianist didn't know the song very well, the microphone went off and on and off, she forgot the words and started over. But long before she came to the end of the song I made a rare discovery about how people who say other people's words can feel about their work. Hearing her bring a lyric to life has become as personal to me as what she is singing about obviously is to her.

She is content with her craft and satisfied to express what she knows about us through it— to sing a song. And—how should I say it?—she knows all about us.

GORE VIDAL
BY TENNESSEE WILLIAMS

THERE IS LESS dissimulation in the brilliant mind of Gore Vidal than almost any other writer-friend I have known. He seems to have none of most writers' apprehensions and timidities in their relation to "The Great Society," he doesn't care what he says nor to whom he says it and he sails along more valiantly all the time with his good looks, his social charm and poise, his wise but tolerant adjustment to "things as they are " in and out of "The G.S." And yet, marvelously, his lighthearted way of going along with the world does not at all make him a conventional artist. His world is never the world of a self-limiting and often self-pitying sensibility. It is the world of a modern Voltaire, and I have heard him publicly declare that he will live to be quite old, and I believe that, if he avoids a plane-crash, he will travel very far indeed, knowing more and more as he goes and saying all that he knows, and saying it wittily, coolly, and memorably.

234

LOUISE BROOKS
BY ANITA LOOS

I FIRST KNEW Louise Brooks in California when she was an early-day sex kitten of the old silent films. At the same time Louise supplied an extremely chic version of the flapper of the Twenties. Her brunette type of good looks had a sort of distinction; bobbed hair was just coming into vogue, but in Hollywood it was generally bleached or tousled in the vulgar manner of Clara Bow, while Louise's had the sleek aristocracy of a young François Premier. Her sophisticated appearance in the razzamatazz hangouts of the film capital brought everything to a standstill. By the same token, Louise's films became conversation pieces in the great outside world; she is still discussed by the movie cultists of Europe.

But during Louise's middle years, when her career as a siren lay behind her, she went through a dramatic metamorphosis and turned into a highbrow. Her very image itself underwent a transformation; Louise became a spare, gray-haired and academic type of intellectual without a trace of her early seduction. Ultimately she established herself in Rochester, New York, where she has developed into a serious writer on the films, their history, their impact on the culture of our times and their validity as works of art.

Louise's two widely different lives have provided her with a unique opportunity to learn the full value of female beauty as opposed to its counterpart, brains. And how does she assess the two? I have an answer in Louise's own words as of July 1965, when she wrote me:

> I remember meeting you on the lot after I'd made a test for Dorothy in *Gentlemen Prefer Blondes* and you said, "Louise, if I ever write a part for a cigar store Indian, you'll get it." This was absolutely right and true. But the older I get, the more I theorize and argue and wave my arms about and I wish I had remained a cigar store Indian.

In effect, Louise, as someone who really knows what she's talking about, might have paraphrased a corny old adage and given it brand-new truth—to wit: Look good, sweet maid, and let who will be clever.

MYRNA LOY
BY ROBERT RYAN

AT SOME POINT in the 1930s custodians of a thing called Vital Statistics were considerably startled by an astonishing rise in the marriage rate. There was no apparent explanation. Nor could a platoon of full-time savants and heavy-duty thinkers come up with one. A great deal of head scratching by anthropologists, sociologists, psychologists *et al* produced practically nothing. It was depression-blighted youth's search for security; it was nature's preparation for another war; it was compensation for the half gainers and swan dives that businessmen were executing from the upper reaches of Wall Street; it was this, it was that. It was nothing of the sort. They just didn't ask the right people.

The right people were young men in their twenties. Like me. And it wasn't population curves or security seeking or biological compensation or any other recondite nonsense. It was the Woman, the Lady, the Wife. It was Myrna Loy. And we all made daily obeisance at her temple. (Three features and a free pack of cigarettes for fifteen cents.) For the first time in the 3,000-year history of the theatre we saw the Ideal Wife. She was haunting but not haunted, witty but not devastating, cool but not cold. She was Florence Nightingale in the sickroom, Madame de Staël in the parlor, Fanny Farmer in the kitchen and Fanny Hill in the hay. She was It. And we rushed out by the hundreds of thousands to find her and marry her. So much for statistics.

Some years later when I had left the movie seat for the movie screen I had the privilege of working with Miss Loy. Unlike the charming and deft William Powell, I had to be a sarcastic, cruel, bitter and savage husband to this vision. Need I say that it took every resource of my limited powers?

Miss Loy today is beautiful, wise, warm, cool, gracious, deeply concerned about her fellow human beings and an adornment of her art.

She hasn't changed a bit.

LICIA ALBANESE
BY ROBERT LEWIS

THOUGHTS FROM THE FRONT ROW . . . February 9, 1965 . . . Albanese's Silver Anniversary performance . . . Carnegie Hall packed for all-Puccini program . . . What will they say? Exquisite, pure, tender singing . . . and *yet* . . . how beautifully she *speaks* the words . . . the diction, the thought behind the phrase . . . like de Luca, Muzio . . . other great ones . . . a compliment to the composer . . . *cantare bene, naturalmente, ma parlare bene* . . . And what will they do? They will scream *brava* and carry on as though Adelina Patti were flaunting her jewels at them and waving her last-but-one Final Farewell . . . and *yet* . . . was ever a prima donna more "businesslike"? . . . a job to do . . . come out, stand ready, deliver fully, inside and out, the sound and meaning . . . just that . . . turn and go . . . no nonsense . . . And what will they write? "On that memorable February 9 in 1940 when Cio-Cio-San, with tiny steps, tripped daintily across the Nagasaki bridge onto the great Metropolitan stage and into the hearts of the audience," etc., etc. . . . and yet . . . in that moment, she knew how to give her self an order, "to enjoy my happiness," and to place that tiny foot carefully, deliver each combined sound-thought-movement unadorned, not pandering . . . then to take the next carefully planned tiny-step and the next and the next . . . right up to this Silver night . . . and on to the Golden one . . . hope I'll be there . . .

GEORGE BURNS
BY GEORGE JESSEL

THE PORTRAIT you see before you is that of a man who has as many talents as he has had names, and likewise as many partners—theatrical partners. He was Brown of Brown and Williams, he was Williams of Williams and Brown, he was Nat Nirnbaum of the Pee Wee Quartet, he was Burns of Burns and Jose, then Burns and Lorraine, Nat Burns, monologist, then finally George N. Burns of Burns and Allen, and this partnership was made in heaven. George was a ballroom dance instructor, a lead singer in quartets on the Bowery, a buck dancer on skates, a stereotyped vaudeville straight man, and the last two decades find him after-dinner speaker *par excellence*, graceful dancer, delightful singer of quaint old songs, and one of the most sophisticated comedians of all time. He's an angel at the dinner table and a Hitler at the bridge table. His two oldest friends in show business are Jack Benny and the writer of this tiny biography, George Jessel, and we love him like a brother.

IRENE SHARAFF
BY WALTER WANGER

. . . her winged shoes to her feete she tied. Formed all of gold
  and all eternified.
That on the round earth or the sea sustained Her ravisht substance
  swift as gusts of wind . . .
Downe from Olympus 'teps she headlong div'd. And swift as thought
  in Ithaca arriv'd.

HOMER, THE ODYSSEY, BOOK I,
lines 161-164; 169-170

IRENE, daughter of the Greeks, divine in her discipline and awareness, dwells in a place inhabited by the gods. Her world is a world of standards and dreams tempered by her understanding of the devices of mortals. Blessed with talent, imagination, integrity and intellect, this inspired spirit of the ancient world is making a contribution that is helping to make our modern world more civilized. All praise to Irene, goddess of beauty!

245

BORIS KARLOFF
BY GEORGE AXELROD

B ACK IN THE good old days when Saturday afternoon movies were thirty-five cents and monsters were monsters (not fun-loving Munsters), you were either a Karloff man or a Lugosi man and that was it. With me it was Karloff all the way. In fact I figured Lugosi was kind of a sissy. The way he kept messing around with girls, biting their necks and stuff.

Actually, I think, there was something about Karloff's monster with which an adolescent boy could make instant identification. I, too, had suddenly become a great bumbling creature, well meaning, God knows, but leaving a continuous wake of havoc and disaster behind me wherever I went.

So strongly did I feel this identication that my first literary effort (at thirteen) was an

attempt to retell the Frankenstein story—this time from the monster's point of view. *It is cold in the tower room where they keep me* [it began]. *My jailer, the Dwarf, carries a flaming torch. I did not ask to be born but now I am afraid to die. I have the brain of a criminal and the face of a monster. They could just as easily have made me handsome. And with this peg in my neck I shall have to have my shirts custom-made . .*

Shortly after that, of course, I fell in love with Alice Faye, and it was not till some years later that my old feelings were rekindled. It was in the early days of television and I had been hired to write something called *The Boris Karloff Mystery Playhouse. Hired?* If they'd only known, they could have had me for nothing.

Anyway—dissolve to the first rehearsal. A silence falls over the gathered actors and technicians as "The Monster" enters the hall. The script (mine) concerned a song-and-dance man with homicidal tendencies (I *told* you this was the early days of television) and required the hero at one point to don a straw hat and perform several choruses of "Mention My Name in Sheboygan." All this was explained to Mr. Karloff in hushed and rather nervous tones. There was another silence. Then, Mr. Karloff sighed, picked up his straw hat, said somewhat wist-

BORIS KARLOFF
BY GEORGE AXELROD

fully, "It's extraordinary what a middle-aged English gentleman will do for money," and went into his number. After that, I don't know about him, but *I* could have danced all night.

The weeks on the *Mystery Playhouse* were pure delight. During rehearsal breaks my hero would frequently ask me to accompany him on brief stalks around the block. And I mean stalks. Boris didn't walk, man, he *stalked!* And we (he) were recognized wherever we went. Faces would pale. Crowds would fall back with hushed gasps: It's *Boris Karloff!* It's *Boris Karloff!* And there was I, right beside him, basking in reflected gory.

Television and I grew older (monsters, of course, are ageless), and I did not see Boris again until a few weeks ago. I had taken a number of my children to lunch at Sardi's. Three adolescent faces suddenly paled and once again I heard that familiar gasp: It's *Boris Karloff!* And sure enough it was. Sitting at a corner table sipping what appeared to be a Beefeater Gibson. "We're old friends," I said, stretching a point a little. "Would you like to meet him?" After a brief consultation three heads shook in the negative. Brought up in an age of Things and Blobs and Creatures From, they still knew a *real* Monster when they saw one.

I must say, I didn't press it. I was a little nervous myself. I mean, hell, it was *Boris Karloff!*

MONTGOMERY CLIFT
BY MARCELLO MASTROIANNI

Those were my moviegoing days. Days when the names James Dean and Marlon Brando still evoked question marks. Yet the true originator of what came to be known as the rebellious twentieth-century anti-hero had already made his entrance. The film was *Red River*, and the restrained performer with the inner tension and those ancient, melancholy eyes was Montgomery Clift.

His presence was so unobtrusively strong that it lingered even when he was off camera. And so I kept going back: *The Heiress, A Place in the Sun, I Confess, From Here to Eternity, The Young Lions*.

And then the distressing news of his accident, the stories of tormented love affairs, his courtships with loneliness, his fits of depression, and his ultimate reclusion. We, colleagues and fans, were all the more saddened because it seemed that all the sympathy in the world could never have helped him.

In a darkened theatre, watching his first film after the accident, I was both curious and apprehensive. Yes, he had changed; the young boy from *Red River* was ten years older. His eyes were reflecting the experience of a lifetime; that ancient melancholy was now tinged with a personal suffering. Yet the presence was still there and still when he was not on screen.

And that was the last film I saw him in, as my moviegoing days are over. Much has happened since: James Dean's career began and abruptly ended, Brandoism has passed its apogee, and perhaps the rebellious anti-hero of our days, to which perhaps I have contributed too, is slightly out of vogue now. But the intensity of Montgomery's eyes, twenty years later, the wisdom of his Etruscan smile, the tragedy of his personal life make him the never-setting expression of our times, the symbol of our difficult duty of living.

250

GEORGE ABBOTT · *1965 New York City*
1988 New York City (101 years old)
LICIA ALBANESE · *1965 New York City*
MARIAN ANDERSON · *1966 New York City*
JULIE ANDREWS · *1961 New York City*
BROOKS ATKINSON · *1965 New York City*
LAUREN BACALL · *1965 Trancas, California*
JACK BENNY · *1965 Los Angeles, guest soloist,*
Los Angeles Philharmonic, conducted by Zubin Mehta.
LEONARD BERNSTEIN · *1965 New York City*
MARLON BRANDO · *1953 New York City*
LOUISE BROOKS · *1965 Rochester, New York*
ERIK BRUHN · *1965 New York City*
GEORGE BURNS · *1965 Hollywood*
RICHARD BURTON · *1962 Rome, Italy*
MONTGOMERY CLIFT · *1954 Stamford, Connecticut*
GLADYS COOPER · *1956 New York City*
AARON COPLAND · *1965 New York City*
FRANCO CORELLI · *1965 New York City*
NOËL COWARD · *1957 New York City*
SAMMY DAVIS, JR. · *1965 New York City*
ALFRED DRAKE · *1960 New York City*
HENRY FONDA · *1956, 1965 New York City*
JANE FONDA · *1965 Malibu, California*
MARGOT FONTEYN · *1965 Hollywood*
JUDY GARLAND · *1963 New York City*
IRA GERSHWIN · *1965 Beverly Hills*
JOHN GIELGUD · *1964 Beverly Hills*
SAMUEL GOLDWYN · *1965 Hollywood*
RUTH GORDON · *1965 Hollywood*
TAMMY GRIMES · *1960 New York City*
JULIE HARRIS · *1956 New York City*
REX HARRISON · *1956 Old Westbury, New York*
LILLIAN HELLMAN · *1965 New York City*
JUDY HOLLIDAY · *1960 New York City*
HEDDA HOPPER · *1963 West Los Angeles, California*
LENA HORNE · *1963 Los Angeles*
CHRISTOPHER ISHERWOOD · *1964 Beverly Hills*
JENNIFER JONES · *1965 Beverly Hills*
BORIS KARLOFF · *1958 Hollywood*
DANNY KAYE · *1965 Beverly Hills*
BUSTER KEATON · *1965 Woodland Hills, California—*
holding a photograph of himself taken in 1900.
KAY KENDALL · *1956 Old Westbury, New York*
BERT LAHR · *1961 New York City*
CHARLES LAUGHTON · *1961 New York City*
MARGARET LEIGHTON · *1965 Hollywood*
JACK LEMMON · *1965 Beverly Hills*
OSCAR LEVANT · *1965 Beverly Hills*
BEATRICE LILLIE · *1965 New York City*
JEAN LOUIS · *1965 Los Angeles*
MYRNA LOY · *1959 New York City*
JOSEPH L. MANKIEWICZ · *1961 Rome, Italy*

MARY MARTIN · *1961 New York City*
GIULIETTA MASINA · *1965 New York City*
ELAINE MAY · *1961 New York City*
MABEL MERCER · *1965 New York City*
ETHEL MERMAN · *1965 New York City*
HENRY MILLER · *1965 Pacific Palisades, California*
PAUL NEWMAN · *1965 Beverly Hills*
MIKE NICHOLS · *1965 Brentwood, California*
RUDOLF NUREYEV · *1965 Hollywood*
LAURENCE OLIVIER · *1964 London, England*
MICHAEL PARKS · *1964 Hollywood*
DONALD PLEASENCE · *1965 Hollywood*
AMANDA PLUMMER · *(frontispiece) 1961 New York City*
CHRISTOPHER PLUMMER · *1965 Stratford, Connecticut—*
as Marc Antony in Julius Caesar.
SIDNEY POITIER · *1966 New York City*
OTTO PREMINGER · *1965 Hollywood*
LEONTYNE PRICE · *1965 New York City*
TERENCE RATTIGAN · *1962 Cannes, France*
ROBERT REDFORD · *1965 Brentwood, California*
LEE REMICK · *1965 Beverly Hills*
CYRIL RITCHARD · *1964 New York City*
JASON ROBARDS · *1959 Cambridge, Massachusetts*
JEROME ROBBINS · *1965 New York City*
EDWARD G. ROBINSON · *1962 Rome, Italy*
MICHAEL ROMANOFF · *1965 Beverly Hills*
DAVID O. SELZNICK · *1965 Beverly Hills*
IRENE SHARAFF · *1961 Rome, Italy*
SIMONE SIGNORET · *1965 Beverly Hills*
PHIL SILVERS · *1965 Beverly Hills*
RED SKELTON · *1965 Hollywood*
OLIVER SMITH · *1965 Brooklyn Heights, New York*
KIM STANLEY · *1957 Hollywood*
MAUREEN STAPLETON · *1959 New York City*
TOMMY STEELE · *1966 New York City*
GEORGE STEVENS · *1963 Page, Arizona*
IGOR STRAVINSKY · *1965 Hollywood*
BARBRA STREISAND · *1963 Hollywood*
ELIZABETH TAYLOR · *1962 Rome, Italy*
DICK VAN DYKE · *1965 Hollywood*
GORE VIDAL · *1964 West Los Angeles, California*
EDWARD VILLELLA · *1965 New York City*
NANCY WALKER · *1953 New York City*
TUESDAY WELD · *1963 New York City*
OSKAR WERNER · *1965 Beverly Hills*
TENNESSEE WILLIAMS · *1965 New York City*
JONATHAN WINTERS · *1964 Beverly Hills*
ESTELLE WINWOOD · *1955 New York City*
1981 Studio City, California (99 years old)
NATALIE WOOD · *1964 Beverly Hills*
ED WYNN · *1963 Page, Arizona—as Blind Old Aram*
in The Greatest Story Ever Told.

Some photographs have been added and others changed since the original publication in 1966 due to damaged or lost negatives or the photographer's personal preferences.

This book was set in Bodoni Book, Bodoni Open and Bauer Bodoni Bold Types by Recorder Typesetting Network, San Francisco. It was printed and bound by Dai Nippon Printing Company, Tokyo, Japan.

The original design of this book was by Paul Bacon and Larry Kamp.
This edition was reformatted and re-created by David Charlsen.